To M___
and ___
with all my
Love and
Wishes of
A great
Creative and
Fun
Life
___

Empowering The Heart

SIMPLE STEPS TO
RESTORE YOUR PEACE, HEAL THE HURT
AND SHARE YOUR GIFTS

BERTRAND BABINET PhD

Poems by Kimberly Jonas

BABINETICS
THE FIVE DYNAMICS OF HEALTH

Ordering Information:
Babinetics, LLC
www.babinetics.com
babinetics@gmail.com
1 (720) 328-8299

Because of the dynamic nature of the Internet, any web addresses or links contained in this book may have changed since publication and may no longer be valid.

The author of this book does not dispense medical advice or prescribe the use of any technique as a form of treatment for physical, emotional or medical problems without the advice of a physician, either directly or indirectly. The intent of the author is only to offer information of a general nature to help you in your quest for emotional and spiritual well-being. In the event you use any of the information in this book for yourself, which is your constitutional right, the author and the publisher assume no responsibility for your actions.

Cover imagery © iStock

ISBN 978-1-7326776-0-9 (sc)
ISBN 978-1-7326776-1-6 (hc)
ISBN 978-1-7326776-2-3 (e)

Library of Congress Control Number: 2018909498

Second Printing 2018
Babinetics, LLC revision date: 11/01/2018

In Praise of *Empowering The Heart*

∽⌒

"We have known Dr. Bertrand Babinet for many years, and this book embodies the wisdom and loving he brings to his healing work. His correlation of psychology, brain research, and Chinese medicine in the metaphor of the Inner Family demonstrates heart-opening insight into the integrative and transformative processes of issue resolution and spiritual growth. The practical exercises—with their focus on Love and Peace—are wonderful tools for *Empowering the Heart*."

H. Ronald Hulnick, Ph.D., and Mary R. Hulnick, Ph.D.
Authors of *Loyalty to Your Soul: The Heart of Spiritual Psychology* and co-directors of the University of Santa Monica Programs in Spiritual Psychology

"Thank you, Bertrand. At last the entire world has an opportunity to receive of your many gifts of healing and what the masters have known about the makings of a blessed life. Your lifetime of research and vast knowledge of the multi-dimensional aspects of body, mind, and spirit brilliantly elucidate the keys to health and happiness. There is wisdom of the ages transmitting from this book."

John Morton, DSS
Author of *The Blessings Already Are* and Spiritual Director of The Movement of Spiritual Inner Awareness

Stillpoint

—

There is a place
within each of us

where we spin so effortlessly,
like a top in perfect balance,
that we seem not to move at all,
simultaneously viewing all directions,
silently absorbing the surrounding expanse.

Where we are neither
stagnant nor asleep,
wakeful in a state of quiet peace
as the insistent chaos of the world
pulses, dances, seduces
with no concept of propriety.

Where our deepest longing lies,
the wellspring of our
passions, dreams and visions,
patiently whispering prayers,
repeating refrains of desire,
that only we can hear and heed.

Where the wisdom of all ages is stored
as perfectly-preserved scrolls,
waiting to be gently dusted
so that the lore that lies within
can at long last be practiced.

CONTENTS

～

FOREWORD

Bertrand has been a gift to me in my life. We ran into each other almost thirty years ago when I had my first healing session with him. His joyful spirit and relaxed calm brought me to a place of peace just from being in his presence. Peace, indeed, is a place of healing. Bertrand himself is a place of peace ... and of joy.

I can tell Bertrand anything. That, for me, is a rare gift. He is one of the most accepting, kind and caring people I know. Years ago I was waiting with Bertrand in a hallway to enter a conference. I revealed to him I was fearful of entering a room filled with hundreds of people, convinced there was something wrong with me because I felt anxious. I was hoping Bertrand would help me see what was off inside me so I could do something about it. He calmly spoke with me, letting me know my sensitivity would indeed be provoked by the situation, having me understand with just a few words that whatever I was experiencing was fine. In that moment I came to peace as I realized I was fine, other than judging that I was not.

There is rarely anything that is not okay with Bertrand. And if it isn't, he works his own tools to get back into peace and joy, where everything is fine and even better than that. This space of peace, which is one of the many gifts of this book, is where transformation can occur.

Bertrand has helped me through hard times, clearing what was in my way so I could respond to my life circumstances from love. When my father was dying, Bertrand helped me resolve old issues so I could truly be with him, fully present in service as he lay dying. Bertrand helped me see how the challenges I had experienced with my father were actually blessings. As a result, I was able to own these gifts and speak my heart while giving the eulogy at my father's funeral.

Bertrand fosters the awareness that to be a peacemaker is a choice to be made over and over again. Once, when I was participating in his "Spirit Focused Leadership" course, I remember hearing him say that some days we might choose the peace process many times throughout the day. We don't just come to peace once but each time we notice we are upset. Upset happens. Now what? Most people will look "out there" to find something to blame for their upset. What if upset just happens. Life can be upsetting. There is nothing wrong with that. Upset can serve as a gift to awaken possibility, especially if the possibility is in becoming a master of choosing peace.

There are threads of Bertrand's teaching through my own work as a transformational and leadership coach. Mastery in life is not about avoiding adversity or challenges, it's about learning life skills so you are resilient, responsive, and resourceful when life does what it does. It's about embracing change while learning so you can meet life on life's terms and win.

When I am coaching a client who is in disturbance, my initial intention is to help quiet their mind and assist them in coming to peace. In peace, there is the ability to see possibility. From possibility we can take actions which move us into creating something new, perhaps even better than before. Now you have turned the upset into a blessing through your willingness to shift to peace and step into new opportunities. Bertrand's work is pivotal in turning upset into blessings, stepping into something more useful and caring. Shifting to peace is a move that accesses our ability to meet life's challenges.

Life isn't joyful because we have glorious circumstances. Life is joyful because we can live in the joy of realizing we are creative beings. We can make things happen. We can see possibility in problems. We can make choices and design something even better than we would have imagined if life circumstances hadn't unfolded the way they did. This book is a practical guide on how to do just that.

Bertrand is not just writing about what he knows. He has used every one of these tools himself, overcoming the challenges he faced, transforming himself in the process, becoming the gift he is today. I continue to be awed when I hear the journey of his life and how he chose to engage in discovering how to live life from peace and joy and then to share what he learned with his students, his clients, and now, with you.

One of my favorite hymns is: "Let there be peace on earth and let it begin with me". If this is something you are called to, this book – overflowing with resources and practical tools – will serve you on your journey of becoming an everyday peacemaker, making a contribution to your own well-being and joy, as well as a gift to us all. May you use it in service to your learning, growth and upliftment. In doing so, we are all blessed.

Leslie Sann, MA, LCPC
Author: *Life Happens: What Are YOU Going to Do About It?*

PREFACE

My Journey as a Modern-Day Shaman

Recently I was in New Zealand and began exploring the healing practices of the Maori. During this process, I revisited my personal journey that has brought me to this place in my life. I was surprised to discover that many aspects of Maori healing practices paralleled the process of my development as a healer.

Key aspects of the old Maori healing ways are still present in the most recent tribal practices as well. These include:

1. A strong focus on the intuitive to identify the causes and treatments of diseases.
2. An awareness that diseases are the result of inner conflicts that reflect a lack of cooperation with the laws of nature. The course of treatment for these includes a healing of memories and the willingness to change our ways.
3. The awareness that past traumas and conflicts are stored in the tissue and structure of the body and that through deep massage, realignment and energy work, those blocks can be released and the natural ability of the body to take care of itself can be restored.
4. A reliance on natural substances to restore balance and health to the body, mind and spirit.

5. A reliance on spiritual support and guidance through invocation, prayer and meditation.

My own developmental path as a healer has followed a similar course. I didn't know that this process would lead me to become a health care practitioner. Rather, I followed an unfolding path that revealed the gifts and talents I had received. I don't remember exactly all the specific steps of my development, but I will cover some key experiences that shaped the way I approach health and healing.

As a young man, I discovered I had an instinctive knowing of the healing abilities of plants. I remember an incident in Normandy where one of my sisters was sick, and after attuning to the imbalance in her body, I held that frequency then went into the fields to find the plant that would restore the balance. Within a short time I discovered the plant and came back home with it. We looked in books to make sure the plant was safe and to know how to use it, and it indeed produced the desired result. This was the beginning of my awareness of my intuitive ability that still forms the cornerstone of all my work.

It took me many more years to explore my intuition and orient myself toward health care as a profession. I began my education by earning degrees in business administration, law, and international relations. These led me to work for the French Embassy for more than seven years. During this time, my personal explorations included humanistic psychotherapy such as Gestalt and Reichian therapy, bioenergetics, primal therapy, Rolfing and several other modalities. I also apprenticed in some of these modalities, and my intuitive ability became more developed.

In 1974 I changed my orientation and moved into full-time healing work. I had completed my training in postural integration, a form of deep connective tissue work similar to Rolfing but with a strong focus on deep emotional release. This became my primary occupation for the next 10 years. I integrated my ability to attune and move energy into this practice and taught this work to many students in the late 1970s and early '80s.

From 1984 to 1987 I studied acupuncture and Chinese medicine and integrated this approach into my practice. I also added a form of chiropractic work called Neural Organization Technique. This allowed me to integrate both the energetic and structural work.

Toward the end of my acupuncture training I began a Ph.D. program in Human Development and graduated in 1989. In each of these new disciplines I incorporated my intuitive awareness, integrating them with one another and creating a body-mind approach with a strong spiritual foundation. I called that work Global Energy Matrix (GEM).

From 1990 to 2000 my focus was primarily on my private practice and GEM trainings, expanding my unique approach to healing, which assists individuals to develop their own healing and intuitive abilities. During that time I gave these trainings regularly throughout the United States, Mexico, South America and Europe. I have recently redesigned this work in two tracks with the same spiritual foundation: one focused on the body, called bio-functional energetics medicine, and the other focused on the psychological aspects of health based on the material in this book, called Spirit Focused Leadership and Transformation.

Following my late wife's diagnosis of breast cancer, my work changed direction again and my focus turned to understanding the biochemistry of the body and the use of plants and supplements to restore physical health. I incorporated those healing modalities into her treatment, and for 10 years she was cancer free. I think that we became somewhat lax in our attentiveness to her health and the cancer came back in multiple areas of her body. The last five years of her life were a time of deep introspection and spiritual focus. Loving and living fully in the moment became the foundation of our lives. At no time did we enter into despair and we used every situation to deepen our understanding of health and healing and our commitment to Spirit and service.

My philosophy of health and healing is based on all my previous experiences. It is one of complete respect for the body and for each person and their uniqueness. I address issues present in the body and in people's lives; however, I do not treat diseases. I treat people. I do this with the greatest compassion, love and caring I can muster. My intuitive ability is at the forefront of my work, but I always back it up with all the scientific information I can find.

Starting during the last five years of my late wife's illness, and continuing today, I have pursued advanced studies in the naturopathic treatment of degenerative disorders, primarily with the Mederi Foundation but also in yearly conferences offered by the Healthy Medicine Academy. The focus is on an integrative approach to health and healing that promises to dramatically transform the practice of medicine.

It is well known at this time that excess weight and obesity have reached a national epidemic level and is a major cause of degenerative diseases. I developed a highly effective weight-loss program and have worked with more than 500 individuals in the ongoing management of their weight. I am discovering the close relationship between trauma, denied self-expression, and the manifestation of chronic excess weight and disease. As we will explore in this book, the body is closely intertwined with our personal effectiveness and every aspect of our psyche. In approaching health and healing it is critical to consider the physical, the psychological and the spiritual.

My work is an integration of everything I have learned. Each year I attend close to a hundred hours of professional training and am a lifelong learner. Beyond my insatiable thirst for knowledge, my prime motivator is to increase my ability to serve the people who come to me for help. I love to serve and I am devoted to always doing the best possible job I can do on their behalf.

I see God as my partner and I am clear that I am simply a channel for the healing process. Unless it is offensive to my clients, my work always starts with an invocation.

A posthumous message from my mother stays present in my consciousness at all times: "The body is the temple of the Soul; it fulfills itself through pleasure, glory and the full expression of our gifts and talents." As we will see throughout this book, the body reflects the various aspects of our consciousness and is the anchor point for the creative imagination, emotions, intellect and the will. As these psychological functions move away from fear, lack and reactivity, and express love, the body progressively releases the negativity and conditioning of the past and becomes a perfect instrument for Divine work. Because love is the essence of all things, when we consciously dedicate ourselves to Spirit, we naturally become purified in the process and the total glory of our Divine endowment becomes manifest through our unique gifts and talents in service to our families, others and the planet as a whole. We will begin our journey exploring the history of what it means to be human, then explore the central place that love occupies in the process of health, healing and personal effectiveness.

MANIFESTATION

No single person writes a book by him or herself, and this one is no exception. It was a collaborative effort from beginning to end. The material emerged from my life experience and I am grateful to all the people who loved, nurtured, guided and challenged me to reach beyond all my limitations. In particular, I must cite my parents and my eleven siblings in France. Also, my forty-seven year marriage with my late wife Roberta, my three sons and their wives, Eric and Lisa, Matthew and Bo, David and Yaakova; as well as their children, Jeremy, Alia, Maxime, Menachem and Rivka.

I also want to thank all the remarkable teachers and mentors that have appeared throughout my life and guided my journey. I especially want to thank my present wife Dani Burke-Babinet who contributes daily to my joy and upliftment. Without all these people I would not be who I am.

I want to thank all the people who contributed to my spiritual growth and my understanding of Love and Peace as the source and the purpose of all existence. In particular, Le Pere Chevignard, a Dominican who inspired my youth, Swami Muktananda, who opened my heart and blew my mind and John-Roger, my teacher, friend and mentor who has been a beacon in my life for the past forty years. All those people have played a unique part in making Love and Peace the center of my existence and work.

I also want to thank all the people who revised my writing, helping me transform the material into a practical essay on how to live in peaceful harmony. Lisa Novick typed, edited and formatted my original dissertation. Dani Burke-Babinet contributed ongoing encouragement and graphic design. Therese Mahannah, my assistant par excellence, cleared my schedule, allowing me time to write. My good friend and dedicated supporter, Tom Boyer described his contribution as translating and editing my "Franglaise" into readable English. My friend and long time collaborator Carol Beau formatted each successive version. My marketing consultant Heather Noto made numerous excellent suggestions. My editor Angela Renkoski reviewed the entire document before sending it for publication.

Last but not least—I want to extend a special thanks to Kimberly Jonas for contributing her poetry and even writing one poem specifically for the book. Kimberly is an amazingly inspired poet and teacher. Her poetry goes to the heart of the human experience.

INTRODUCTION TO
EMPOWERING THE HEART

Most of us have experienced major challenges in our upbringing. Family, cultures, religion, trauma, etc., have left scars in our willingness to trust, our self-confidence, self-concept and self-image. These limitations impair our ability to be fully present in our lives, as well as restrict the full expression of our unique gifts and talents in service to ourselves, others and the world. This book offers a series of strategies to assist you in moving beyond these imaginary blocks and invites you to release your brakes and embrace a destiny of joyful upliftment.

Our brains and bodies have been programmed to survive and to seek the fulfillment of our needs outwardly. The common results are fear and a sense of lack. Breaking instinctive defense mechanisms is our first task in restoring personal freedom. The primary key in this pursuit is the empowerment of the heart.

The Spiritual Heart is where the Spirit touches the flesh. Opening the heart is the prerequisite for willingness and receptivity so major positive change can occur and be sustained. You can cancel reactivity, discover Inner Peace in any circumstance, and access deep spiritual love within as well as discover the hidden keys of spiritual fulfillment.

You will also explore how we have been programmed and how to free yourself from conditioned responses. Many people do not want to look inward and discover their limitations, preferring to deny what is going on or justifying dysfunctional behaviors by blaming others for their life circumstances.

For those who do want to live freely, exploring the meandering realities of our deep programming requires the light of the Soul. The Spiritual Heart is a point of access of that necessary inner light we want to be able to turn to at will.

This book is for those with the courage and willingness to undertake the challenging and ultimately deeply rewarding journey of becoming fully human. To guide you in navigating the necessary terrain of the psychological functions of the brain, I offer a map I call the "Inner Family."

The Inner Family clarifies four specific dynamics that impact every action in our lives. These dynamics are:

- Preservation
- Authenticity
- Wisdom
- Contribution

The Dynamics of the
INNER FAMILY

MOTHER	FATHER
Function of Preservation	**Function of Authenticity**
Taking care	Direction
Support	Integrity
Teaching	Commitment
Nurturing	Flow
Protecting	Authority
	Intention

GRANDPARENTS	CHILD
Function of Wisdom	**Function of Contribution**
Organization	Exploring
Process	Creating
Learning	Discovering
Knowledge	Growing
Experience	
Method	

© 2016 Babinetics, LLC.

Because of frequent dysfunction in our family or traumatic life events, these basic functions were often not supported in the most effective ways. As a result, we were left with reactive mechanisms that greatly impact our happiness and personal effectiveness. We will explore the Inner Family as a whole and the specific roles played by each member. We will examine not only their magnificent purpose in our consciousness but also how they can be applied for healing, growth and upliftment in our everyday lives.

Issues in our lives reflect to us where the needs for expansion lie. We do not react to things we know how to handle. Every issue is an opportunity to expand our consciousness, becoming more authentic and more resourceful. The useful pattern is:

1. Identify where the restriction is.
2. Restore Inner Peace.
3. Heal the hurt.
4. Use our spiritual connection to mobilize our inner resources.
5. Take actions that move us toward the highest good of all concerned.

This requires all the positive attributes of the Inner Family: caring and compassion (Mother), clarity of purpose and values (Father), the willingness to learn (Grandparents) and creative imagination and daring (Child).

Inner peace and love are the foundation for this profound work of healing. This book will help you identify your limitations and discover ways to use them as a springboard for your upliftment.

All of our negative patterns are, at heart, a search for love. As you discover and embrace the love within, those limitations will drop away and you will create harmony and balance within yourself.

Because health is contagious, you will experience your zone of influence expanding in positive and uplifting ways. As your ability to share and express unconditional loving expands, it will become the foundation of great abundance and responsible contribution in your life. I wish you all the best on this magnificent heart-empowering journey!

Touching God

—

Every day, bless the ground
on which you walk.
Speak reverence to the
hallowed earth that
quivers with each step
of your querying soul,
absorbs the shockwaves of
your wild dance of discovery,
cradles the soles of your feet
over millions of seeking miles,
steadies you from below
with supple strength
so that you may be certain
of touching God.

Chapter One

UNDERSTANDING THE HUMAN DILEMMA

Between Heaven and Earth

SPIRIT
Active
We Connect to Spirit through the Heart.

	H	
Mother Preservation Connective	U	**Father** Authenticity Directive
Grandparents Learning Cognitive	M A N	**Child** Expression Creative

© 2016 Babinetics, LLC.

THE WORLD
Attractive
We Connect to the World through the Brain and the Senses.

The Historical Background

Many spiritual traditions have referenced two movements in the human consciousness. One is a "higher" nature, seeking fulfillment through self-control, altruism and moral integrity. The second is a "lower" nature seeking instant gratification through pleasure and narcissism. Various explications have been offered to explain this dichotomy, such as the "Fall" in Judaism and Christianity. Beyond this, many traditions of the East and West have sought elevation and liberation through abnegation and asceticism. All of those traditions have something in common: the notion that the spiritual quest for transcendence is "good" and that in some way the material world is "bad." This has transformed our relationship between the spiritual and the material as an either/or and a struggle between heaven and hell. They also often associate women with temptation and the cause of our separation from the Spiritual. The result has been the creation of a male-dominated hierarchical structure throughout most societies.

Heaven, Earth and Man

The Chinese model offers a relationship between the spiritual and material that is both integrative and transformative. The metaphorical "Heaven" is seen as active, meaning it is present and in a state of flow. This is the quality described as Yang. The metaphorical "Earth" is perceived as attractive or receptive, inviting us outward. This quality is called Yin. "Man" is placed in the middle. Notice that there is no judgment involved, just a description of a state of affairs that explains our dual nature.

The spiritual is looking upward to Heaven for our fulfillment and outward to Earth for our gratification and opportunities to participate in the fullness of our expression.

Our quest is to be open to receive spiritually from Heaven through increased awareness of the ongoing flow of Spirit. By allowing spiritual empowerment, we enhance our fulfillment so that our relationship to the world can become less needy or attached and more devoted to caring service.

A metaphor that I often use to describe our special "Man" or human role is a water hose. We connect the hose to the Source (Heaven), open to the flow, then water the garden (Earth), attending to the beauty of life and participating in the dance of nature.

Connecting to the Source and learning how to maintain alignment is our primary job, which we will explore in depth in this book. We will also explore a major key in allowing the flow of Spirit: letting go of judgment and moving into forgiveness, thus constantly reconnecting to the Source. How to cancel or dissolve our reactivity, thus empowering our expression toward service, is offered through the metaphor I have termed the "Inner Family."

Connection to Spirit Through the Heart

The scientific and medical worlds tend to look at the heart as a pump that moves the blood around. Mystical traditions around the world, however, have always revered the heart as the connection to Spirit. When people are deeply moved by a loving expression, they naturally respond to that openness by touching the center of the chest. The human heart starts pumping in the embryo about 21 days before, and independently of, the development of the nervous system. Maybe this is the reason the heart brings a greater sense of connectedness to Spirit while the brain has evolved to address survival issues and tends to be more reactive and connected to the Earth. The beating heart transports nutrients throughout the embryo, allowing growth and maturation of the rest. We know that children who are denied physical expression of love and caring after birth are stifled in both their physical and psychological development. My own biofeedback research has also shown that the experience of Inner Peace by focusing on the heart harmonizes the brain and strengthens the organs of the body. It is the heart of "Man" that is the centerpoint of "Heaven" and "Earth."

Connection to the World Through the Brain

The brain is designed to cope with the external environment. It is conditioned and molded based on how effectively basic needs were addressed in our childhood as well as inherited traits from our genetics and culture. There are four primary "parts" or aspects to our brain. The oldest is our "reptilian" brain, which focuses on the need for safety and security. The need for caring and connection affects our limbic brain. Needs that relate to understanding affect our cognitive (left hemisphere) brain, and needs that correspond to creative expression affect our creative (right hemisphere) brain. Any trauma or lack in the foundational development of these parts of our brain results in a sense of lack and fear that promotes reactivity.

In contrast to other animals, humans are born with very little survival means of our own. Humans are highly dependent for many years on our external environment for all our basic needs. It is easy for us to become dependent on our support system if it is overly attentive. Or we may become somewhat narcissistic or feel very deprived if our family system is deficient in our early years. We also may develop patterns of separation or distrust. The outward-looking senses (Yin) look for gratification, and overindulging those senses can create imbalances while deprivations can create strong cravings.

In either case the result is that our fear of lack disconnects us from our heart, which is our authentic empowerment. As we disconnect from the Source, we seek compensatory gratifications through the movement of our ego. Deficiency in security promotes an ego need for control. Deficiency in caring generates an ego need for approval. Lack of appreciation for our innate curiosity as a child promotes a sense of being misunderstood and an ego need for recognition. A lack of support for our creative expression results in an ego need for attention. Those deficiencies are the basis of most dysfunctional behaviors and patterns of reactivity.

We will explore in detail the expression of these different functions of the brain in the model of the Inner Family. Learning how to move beyond reactivity by empowering the heart is the foundation of authentic empowerment and the key to happiness. We will explore how to reconnect to the heart as the foundation for authentic empowerment.

Spread the Word

—

*There is one
special ingredient
that propels life forward,
gives us the wisdom
and unbridled power
required to release
judgment, fear,
blame and skepticism,
tap the brilliance
we are capable of,
rediscover connection
to divine flow.*

*This is not a
secret ingredient.
One that has to be
mentioned in
hushed voices,
squirreled away,
hoarded to avoid
over-use.*

*It is to be
celebrated with
a clear, vibrant voice
that hides nothing,
shares everything,
an ingredient
to be used liberally,
spread far and wide
without equivocation:*

LOVE.

Chapter Two

LOVE AS A HEALING AND TRANSFORMATIONAL PROCESS

~

The Heart of the Matter

Many traditions from Jesus to the Buddha have talked about the heart as the foundation for our spiritual transformation. Recent research indicates that there are 40,000 neurons in the heart involved in complex communication with the brain. The electromagnetic field of the heart is 600 times more powerful than the field of the brain. Changes in our state of consciousness due to fear and lack, or toward peace and joy, are immediately received by the infants and animals around us and impact their behavior.

Recent research at the HeartMath® Institute shows that heart coherence (or what I call Inner Peace) instantly harmonizes the brain, balances our neurological system, reduces stress in our body, and improves organ and immune functions. We are going to explore how to connect to Inner Peace as a doorway to spiritual love. This is why I have made peace and love the very foundation of my work and my life.

For many people the word *love* suggests romance, relationships and courting, and many authors have explored love from that point of view, creating plays, poems, novels and research documents on love and various aspects of relationship. Typical titles in that category are concerned with: How do we fall in love? How do we stay in love? What makes good relationships?

Others explore love within the context of sexuality, and their concern is with lovemaking, which for the most part ought to be called "various ways of expressing our sexuality."

Another dominant theme is love and spirituality. This content is along the lines of what to do or not do in order to deserve God's love and, by extension, anyone's love.

I am looking at love as the integrating process, the connecting principle of all things and all people, more in line with a spiritual approach to life. However, this book is not a philosophical essay on love, the importance of love or the nature of love. It is a practical guide to the healing and transformational power of love—how to get in touch with it, sustain it, and apply it to specific aspects of our lives. Love is easily accessible and profoundly enriching when we place it in the center of our lives.

This book presents a developmental framework of health and wellness, inspired by Indian and Chinese traditions as well as trends in holistic healing, which bridges the gap between Eastern and Western practices. It is comprehensive, relatively simple and practical.

The practice of living love does not violate any religious creeds and often makes sense to many who profess no spiritual inclination. My hope is that by sharing this framework and specific strategies, individuals will have the ability to deal with life challenges in a more harmonious and loving way. This book is intended to inspire people to make loving the central focus of their lives and of their work.

When people move beyond their fears and truly open their hearts, a deep process of healing and transformation begins that reaches beyond the individuals themselves, touching everyone and everything in their surroundings. Love is a powerful source of healing, wisdom and harmony. Connecting with love makes us stronger, more self-supporting, and less likely to fall into dependency patterns. So, how can we move from reactivity promoted by fear and lack toward reconnection to the Inner Peace that allows spiritual love to flow?

Inner Peace is the foundation for connecting to the love within each human being. I look at the heart and Inner Peace as the doorway and loving as the spiritual flow that promotes authentic empowerment. A way of describing this dynamic is:

When there is peace, there is love.
When there is love, there is oneness.
When there is oneness, there is fulfillment.

Connecting with the Love Within

Love has traditionally been associated with touching—probably due to the unique role that touching plays in the special relationship between mother and child. Human beings crave touching, unless seriously traumatized or born with grave abnormalities. Touching is a way of transcending the separation of our bodies and sharing intimacy and oneness. Touching is, in fact, so much the language of love, that when we want to indicate that anything has reached our heart in a caring way, we simply say, "I was touched." Whether it's in French, German, Spanish, Italian or Russian, identical expressions are used to indicate that the heart is reached in a caring way. This universality to the language of the heart points the way to a strategy for reconnecting with our heart whenever we seem to lose that connection. Another curious reality is that when we say, "I was touched," we instinctively bring our hand to the center of our chest. Because this place in the body is associated with the Spiritual Heart, it is that location of the heart, rather than the physical heart, that I refer to here.

Inner Peace—the Doorway to Spiritual Empowerment

There are a few contexts that help us connect to our Inner Peace, restoring our inner flow. I call them symbols of peace because the origin of the word symbol means "to bring together." The following five symbols of peace can help us connect with our Inner Peace.

- Nature
- Music
- Pets
- Babies
- Focusing on or touching the center of the chest

This information can give us practical help in becoming more connected with our love. It is generally assumed that we learn love from people, primarily from our mothers. We also learn to love in many other situations in our lives. It is important to know this because some people have had rather disastrous childhoods and might falsely conclude that they have no hope of ever learning how to love.

Not all of these symbols will work for everyone in restoring the connection to the heart. However, among the thousands that I have worked with, I have never found anyone who was not sensitive to at least one of these five symbols. The following exercise will help identify which symbol or symbols will best work for you.

Symbol Exercise

Recall any situation in which you felt particularly touched involving one of the four catalysts—nature, music, pets, or babies—or simply focus on and touch the center of your chest. This will instantly connect you with your heart. Since we know that the heart is the seat of love and oneness, we naturally access these resources when we connect with profound experiences of being touched. The sharper the memory and intensity of the experience, the more intense the connection with the heart will be.

Most of the time, the experience of being in touch with our heart is subtle, peaceful and undramatic. At times, the experience may be ecstatic. However, in our search for this transcendental experience, we often miss a profound and no less transforming, subtle reality. Love does not always come with lots of fanfare.

Probably one of the greatest difficulties for some in connecting with love is its simplicity and peacefulness. In a world where so much is designed to stimulate our senses, it is easy to misjudge the power of love because of its subtle, simple quality.

Reconnecting with Love Exercise

Here is the entire approach to reconnecting with love, which you can practice, step by step, until the process becomes familiar and easily attainable.

1. Focus on nature, music, a pet, a baby, or put your hand on your heart. If you feel very emotional or attached to the image you first choose, try something else that touches you deeply but that you feel more neutral about.

2. Identify how this makes you feel. Is the feeling peaceful, harmonious and expansive?

3. Realize that you are the source of that feeling; it is coming from within you, not from the external element that triggered it.

4. To claim control and power over this feeling, practice increasing it, expanding it, and discovering how many different ways you can play with this feeling.

5. Send the feeling to your hands, your feet, any place in your body that feels constricted and that might need love for any reason, such as hurt, guilt, shame, painful memories and so forth and or extend it to any relationship or situation you want to bring into greater balance

6. Return to the reference point that triggered the love anytime you feel the connection is lost. This is very important because you will learn that it is within your power to bring it back.

To fully experiment with the power of love, it is useful to become very familiar with this approach. Practice it daily as a form of meditation. Use this technique to bring love and peace into any area of your life that could use healing or improvement. Bring love into your body for greater health; into your relationships for harmony, growth and fulfillment; and into your work for balance, clarity of purpose and effectiveness. Bring it into every aspect of your life until it not only becomes second nature to you but first nature. When this approach is practiced regularly, it has a profound impact on a person's life.

Healing the Body

In dealing with bodily conditions, start with the Reconnecting with Love Exercise above and direct the Spiritual Love as if it were a jet of energy into any area that needs attention. There is an instantaneous strengthening or cleansing process that occurs. This does not mean that the condition has been cured or will not reoccur, but by breaking up the negative field of energy around the area and bringing forward a natural integrative force, the healing process can be greatly enhanced.

I have also discovered that by teaching this technique to my clients, we work much more cooperatively during our sessions. When clients continue the healing process on their own between appointments, the recovery period is shortened substantially.

Dealing with Conflicts

This technique is especially helpful in dealing with conflicts and situations that tend to promote, prolong or exacerbate separation.

Start with the Reconnecting with Love sequence. Use your symbol to connect to the peace to restore the loving flow. Extend that love to the situation or bring the situation into the flow of loving. Observe the changes as they take place inside you. You do not have to like the situation. You simply want to let go of reactivity so you can reclaim your personal power and deal with the situation more clearly and creatively.

Occasionally, this is enough to relieve the negativity and put the situation in perspective to deal with it more appropriately.

Often though, there is an attachment to the negativity, and it is difficult to maintain the positive energy promoted by the symbol of peace that you chose. In such a case, focus on the positive love-producing symbol of peace while inhaling, and focus on the disturbing situation while exhaling. In most instances, within a few minutes you will experience a major transformation in your feelings toward the situation and a willingness to approach it in a more balanced way.

The time it takes to release negativity seems to be directly proportional to the degree of attachment anyone has in being right. It is amazing how invested in our negativity we can get when we have decided that we are right. Most of the time, this conviction of how right we are is practically a guarantee we are looking at the situation without clarity, creativity or compassion, and certainly with an absence of neutrality. A precious saying that I love that I have heard attributed to Fritz Perls, the creator of Gestalt Therapy, is, "In life, you can either be right or be happy but not both, so choose." Connecting to the heart and the love within is a great way to be happy.

One of the first times I had an opportunity to share with my friend and mentor John-Roger, the creator of the Movement of Spiritual Inner Awareness, I told him, "John-Roger, I do not understand most of the esoteric knowledge you share with us. One of the things I have dedicated my life to is Loving. Is that enough?" He replied, "Bertrand, I do not know if this is enough, but I can guarantee you two things: First, you will always be happy; second, it will always lead you naturally to your next spiritual step." After more than 40 years of spiritual studies I have acquired a great deal of esoteric knowledge, but to this day, what I am fully clear about is that the foundation of spiritual transformation is simply loving (connecting to the Source of love within and extending it to everyone and everything in our life).

Identifying Powerful Inner Resources

One of the keys to personal effectiveness is learning how to connect to our intuition to access our inner resourcefulness. The qualities that empower us are all aspects of Love, our spiritual essence. Qualities such as strength, courage, humor, joy, cooperation, patience, gentleness, and flexibility are aspects of love. Each of these is a particular resource that can apply to specific situations.

Identifying the quality or qualities that improve personal effectiveness in a specific context can assist us in becoming much more effective in the way we handle challenging situations. Some individuals are very good at identifying these positive qualities simply by accessing their intuition and asking themselves, "What quality would best assist me in handling this situation gracefully and effectively?" For others, the list below might assist them in identifying clear inner resources that apply to a specific situation. All those qualities have one thing in common; each one has a natural empowering frequency. This is not an exhaustive list, and with practice, I am sure you will discover new words you will want to add to the list.

Process for Using Empowering Qualities

A
Abundance
Acceptance
Alertness
Appreciation
Articulate
Authenticity

B
Balance
Beauty
Boldness
Brightness
Brilliance

C
Caring
Clarity
Commitment
Competence
Cooperation
Courage
Creativity

D
Daring
Decisiveness
Delight
Diligence
Directness
Discernment
Drive

E
Ease
Elegance
Empathy
Enthusiasm
Excellence
Expressive

F
Faith
Faithfulness
Fidelity
Forgiveness
Freedom
Friendship
Fun

G
Giving
Generosity
Gentleness
Glory
Grace
Gratitude

H
Happiness
Healing
Holiness
Honesty
Honor
Hope
Humor

I
Innocence
Intelligence

J
Jolly
Joy
Jubilation
Justice

K
Kindness
Knowing

L
Leadership
Leniency
Lightheartedness
Lightness
Love
Luck

M
Magnificence
Mastery

N
Neutrality
Nurturing

O
On-task
On-point
Openness
Opportunity

P
Patience
Peace
Persistence
Perseverance
Playfulness
Precision

R
Radiant
Receptivity
Regal
Reflective
Rejoicing
Relaxation
Resilience
Resonance
Resourcefulness
Respect
Reverence
Response-ability

S
Sacredness
Sensibility
Sensitivity
Spirited
Solemnity
Strength
Supportiveness

T
Tenderness
Trust
Trustworthy
Truthfulness

U
Understanding
Upliftment

V
Vibrance
Vigilance
Vivacity
Vulnerability

W
Willingness
Wisdom

Y
Youthfulness

Z
Zeal
Zest

Empowering Qualities Exercise

This exercise is usually integrated at the end of a clearing process using Inner Peace to cancel reactivity. Once you have reached neutrality you would identify a positive quality or qualities that can assist you in moving forward. Then you would follow the sequence below. You can focus on a challenging situation and do this right now.

Internalizing the Qualities

- Take a moment to take in each useful quality in the same way we did with peace and love.
- Do not get caught up in the mental meaning of the quality.
- Look at it as a powerful inner energy that you want to receive in a greater way to assist you with the situation.
- Connect to the quality, receive it, absorb it, enjoy it and become one with it as best as you are able.

Externalizing the Quality

- Once you have identified the key inner resources, check and notice what they would bring to the situation that challenges you.
- Do this one quality at a time as you learn this technique. With practice you can do this with all the qualities at once.

> - The following questions may assist you:
>   - If I was approaching this situation with this quality, how would it look?
>   - How would I feel about the situation?
>   - How would I describe the situation?
>   - What new action or actions would I take to address the issue?

Sometimes when I am apprehensive about dealing with a challenging client, I focus on the heart and come back into the peace, internalizing it and accessing the flow of love. Then I extend it to the situation. When I am back into my neutrality and loving, I ask what quality would be most useful in the situation. In one situation, for example, I was preparing myself for an appointment with someone who consistently challenged every suggestion I made. She wanted instant results and did not understand that healing is a process, and that the result does not happen by magic but by full participation. The quality I identified doing the exercise was trust. I realized that my client had a deep trust issue and wanted to be reassured that her effort would be rewarded and I was not leading her in the wrong direction. Her doubt was promoting impatience in me and I was not communicating the trust I had in the outcome.

My work with her after I completed my process was focused on staying in the trust and in giving her specific signposts to watch for in her process of recovery. As I did that, her participation improved and with greater involvement she gained greater control over the process and progressively started seeing and acknowledging all the ways her health and wellbeing were improving.

Other qualities that have shown up at different times were gentleness, patience, clarity, flexibility, trust, persistence, and firmness. I then internalize the quality or qualities, seeing myself using them in my interaction with my clients. Invariably, I feel a qualitative shift internally and my attitude changes as I go into the situation from a place of authentic empowerment. Most of the time my clients experience the change in my attitude toward them and come into great cooperation and trust in their ability to achieve optimal health.

When you change your attitude you change your experience. When you raise your altitude on any given situation you see it with a new attitude. I have found that this little exercise lets me connect with uplifting qualities, which then changes my reactive attitude to a willingness to serve. That invariably transforms the situation into an opportunity for learning and growth. That serves both my client and me, leading to results that fall in the category of "for the highest good of all concerned."

Healing Past Memories

Many of us carry many memories of past situations that were traumatic. We tend to create ineffective internal patterns around these memories, such as hurt, fear, anger, guilt, resentment and sadness. These patterns limit and decrease our personal power and our ability to get what we want and deserve. Regular use of the appropriate symbol or symbols of peace will bring a greater level of neutrality into what has happened in the past and enables us to extract profound learning from disturbing circumstances.

Healing Past Memories Exercise

In dealing with hurtful memories, the process is similar to the one described above.

- Choose one painful memory at a time.
- Using the symbol of peace you've chosen, access the neutrality and direct the loving to that specific incident.
- Focus on the symbol while inhaling, and on the memory you want to balance while exhaling. This will prevent your getting caught up in the charge associated with the situation and losing track of the purpose of the exercise, which is to mobilize love as a source of healing and integration.
- It is not unusual for this approach to initiate a substantial amount of emotional release. As it comes up, be gentle with yourself, allowing the releasing process, realizing that the hurt is being moved out to restore your strength and freedom of expression.

Living Love

While the technique is quite simple and effective, bringing love into every aspect of our lives is not always easy. While love is a very natural process, many distortions in our education and culture affect our ability to access living love. Prejudices, judgments and the desire to stand out and to get ahead all tend to make us forget that we are part of one living organism in which cooperation plays a major role for survival.

The patterns of lack we developed in our childhood, or possibly that we were born with, act as profound driving forces that tend to push us away from the path of the heart. Our need to please, to seek approval, recognition, security, and attention are all clamoring to tell us in some distorted way that the secret to our fulfillment is somewhere "out there." "If only I could get that person to love me, I would know that I am worthwhile. If only I could get that next degree . . . that next book published . . . that higher professional award, I will have finally shown them who I am. If only I had more money, more possessions, more children, more power, I would finally know that I am secure. If only I could find an audience big enough, attentive enough, refined enough, I would know that I matter and that I am important." Etc., ad nauseam.

Society, families, work, and cultural organizations all reward these negative ego drives and maintain the illusion that we are getting closer to our goals of love, happiness and joy. People in top consulting firms have a name for that process; they call it "the golden shackles." However, for many of us the pursuit of an unreachable goal feels more like a nightmare.

Looking outwardly for what has always been inside promotes more and more hurt. A sense of rejection, abandonment, betrayal and disappointment may start to pervade our lives. Slowly, sometimes imperceptibly, we close our hearts. Not only do we adversely affect our relationships with others, we also seriously hurt our relationship to ourselves. Even more devastating, we block our relationship to God because in the heart these are all one and the same. In a strange way, the more we need love, the more we tend to close the source from which it springs. In our stubbornness, we do not realize that the love we think we receive from other people, or from nature, or from a pet or anything else is already within us.

Our feelings emerge from within ourselves. We cannot experience anything for which we do not have a reference point within. Musicians already have the music within them. They may need good instruments and external stimulation to bring out the right mood, but the music already exists within them waiting for an opportunity. In the same way, the heart, like all of our centers, is often being played by external circumstances.

Because of this, there are times we do not recognize that the music of our heart comes from within ourselves. Love is like beautiful music; it can be strong, subtle, tender, confrontational and much more. It can express all the potentialities of our own being, but it always emerges from the heart. Unlike a musical instrument, we do not need an external musician to play us. We can produce the beautiful music of the heart ourselves. As we can all speak and sing, we can all love. Some of us may be more proficient, but with practice we can all improve.

Many of us were fortunate to have healthy primary teachers of love in our parents. Yet, even then there were times we did not get all that we wanted and we closed down, forgetting how beautiful it was to love.

For others, what they learned from their parents violated the heart and degraded the knowledge of their inner beauty. This might have ranged from upsetting to tragic, but it is not irreversible. Many things in the world speak the language of love and can touch us deeply. As we acknowledge anything that touches us, we start a movement in our consciousness that naturally teaches us how to love. Becoming aware of each experience of love is one way to learn how to play the instrument of the heart and compose our song of love. That song is the expression of our uniqueness, and sharing it with others is the natural fulfillment of our destiny.

Love is a totally self-sufficient dynamic that pervades and sustains everything in the universe. Loving—the act of being aware of that oneness and living our lives in that consciousness—is a practice. It requires a minute-by-minute conscious choice so as not to get caught in the illusion of separation.

The four psychological functions of the brain help us manage every situation in our lives. These are the ability to connect, to direct, to learn and to imagine. These four functions are not static and form a dynamic interplay within our brain in relationship to our environment. For this reason, I like to call them dynamics to reflect their ongoing movement in a complex equilibrium. Because they are so closely linked to the members of the family in which we were raised, I see them globally as the Inner Family and refer to each one of them as a family member.

I associate the connecting function with the Mother and call those dynamics Preservation; the directing function with the Father, I call Authenticity; the learning function of the Grandparents are the dynamics of Wisdom; and imagining is associated with the Child and I call those dynamics Contribution. With the dynamics of the heart in loving, they form the foundation of five powerful dynamics, which we will explore in detail in the following chapters.

There is a profound aspect of the human journey that affects us in every aspect of our lives. Human beings are designed for flow and ease but programmed in fear, lack and reactivity. The Chinese tradition calls this Heaven and Earth, and it is the foundation of their understanding of health. I call it Spirit, the World and You, or as I have said, "the water hose approach to enlightenment."

As we connect to the heart through Inner Peace, we also connect to the flow of love that empowers our expression in service to ourselves as well as others. The Inner Family dynamics are the foundation that allows us to become peacemakers and caretakers when we choose love as the foundation of our lives.

The Potter's Wheel

—

We are not
cast in stone.

We were not imagined
as a form made from
marble or limestone,
alabaster or onyx,
rigid, immutable gestures
made of a finite number of
chiseled angles,
never changing,
never growing.

We were all conceived
to become the unimaginable.

To take our place on the potter's wheel,
unknown twists and turns
unfolding on themselves,
our soft, supple form
shaping and reshaping
from a malleable, undefined shape
into vibrant expressions
never before seen.

To embrace our many incarnations
as an essential part of creative evolution,
all illusion of mastery or consummation
shattered by the grace of our
limitless shape shifting.

To surrender the comfort of
what we believe to be
the pièce de résistance,
our final opus immortalized by
fierce attachment.

To fold back in on ourselves
and begin again,
the wisdom of old forms intact,
firmly rooted in our cells,
though never holding us hostage,
never cured to the bone.

Chapter Three

THE DYNAMICS
OF THE INNER FAMILY

~⌒

Now that we have learned how to restore the heart to its primary role, let's focus on how to use this approach to heal the Inner Family. The Inner Family is a metaphor to describe the four psychological functions of the brain: connecting, directing, learning, and imagining. The word "dynamics" signifies an interplay of forces that defines movement or equilibrium. Obviously, the brain is not static, and different parts of the brain work together in interactive ways to assist us in managing various domains of activities, life challenges and opportunities. In a similar way, members of a family may have different functions and challenges but all participate in the health or the dysfunction of the family unit. Each function of the brain is developed through interplay of life experiences and is greatly influenced by the family in which we were raised. Challenges in the family are often reflected in the children, directly impacting the ability to use these four functions of the brain effectively.

As we have seen, our life is managed through Five Functions, four associated with the brain (connecting, directing, learning and imagining) and one, Loving, associated with the heart and aligned with our spiritual source that promotes Inner Peace and integration.

- **Connecting** is the process, through our emotions, in which we become aware of and tend to our needs and those of other people and our physical environment. This caring function preserves our wellbeing and the wellbeing of the life around us. These dynamics are directly associated with the role of the Inner Mother and Preservation.

- **Directing** or guiding is the role of the Inner Father. This is the ability of the will to line up with our values, lead us on a course of purpose, and search for truth. This dynamic follows our progression through higher and higher levels of motivation and self-expression. It finds its highest function when we align our will with the Divine will. I call the dynamics here Authenticity.

- **Learning** is the ability to understand the working of things, people and all aspects of life and turn our life experiences into wisdom. It is the role of the Inner Grandparents. I call this ongoing thirst for knowledge the dynamics of Wisdom.

- **Imagining** is the ability through which children can transcend the limitation of the social environment and discover the uniqueness of their gifts, talents, affinities and interests. These are the dynamics of the Inner Child. They are throughout our lives that moves us beyond limitations toward greater contribution. I call these dynamics Contribution.

To review, these four tools of life management—connecting, directing, learning, and imagining—operate in the brain, so

I refer to them as functions. In their operational context of personal growth and development in the Inner Family, we go through our life moving toward higher and higher realization, so I call them dynamics. They are Preservation, Authenticity, Wisdom and Contribution. I have chosen those names to indicate their higher purpose. When they are aligned with the heart, they promote expansion and fulfillment. When they are caught in lack or materialism, they promote contraction and ego identification.

The Dynamics of the
INNER FAMILY

MOTHER	FATHER
Function of Preservation	**Function of Authenticity**
Taking care Support Teaching Nurturing Protecting	Direction Integrity Commitment Flow Authority Intention
GRANDPARENTS	CHILD
Function of Wisdom	**Function of Contribution**
Organization Process Learning Knowledge Experience Method	Exploring Creating Discovering Growing

© 2016 Babinetics, LLC.

Attributes of the Four Members of the Inner Family

If love dominates, the Inner Family is functional, happy, healthy and full of love. If fear and coercion dominate, the Inner Family is dysfunctional and full of contradictions, negative feelings and destructive behaviors. Most of the time it is neither totally one nor the other but a combination of both.

Understanding more clearly the dynamics of the Inner Family often sheds light on physical dysfunctions and suggests mental/emotional strategies to assist in the treatment of chronic disorders.

Each member of this internal family has its unique characteristics, function and relationship to the other members. Each has negative tendencies anchored in lack and fear along with beautiful qualities with which they are naturally endowed and that fully express our spiritual purpose. Our Inner Family often reflects the parenting we received as we grew up and the social and circumstantial influences that impacted that parenting. It is also influenced by our in utero experience as well as our genetic characteristics and possible karmic needs.

Let's look more closely at the symbolic characteristics of the dynamics and how we can use each to empower ourselves.

The Mother

In many traditions, the Mother dynamic is associated with the Earth. Mother Earth is the provider bringing forward what is necessary to meet our needs. Primarily Mother Earth, directly or indirectly, supplies food, shelter, clothing and life experiences from which we can learn and grow. The Earth is not only the provider but also the teacher. Being receptive to its teaching is critical for survival. Learning from the Earth is part of the common human wisdom. The Mother, because of her unique caring function, is most attuned to the needs of her environment.

The Influence of Our Mother

Our relationship with our mother is symbiotic in the first year of our life. Our perception of self is greatly determined by the closeness of the connection our mother had with herself, with us, and with her ability to respond to our needs. This quality of bonding with our mother in large part defines our self-esteem and our ability to give or receive love. This becomes the foundation for our own ability to connect and form strong social bonds. This basic connective ability is predicated on respect, responsibility, the ability to take care of ourselves and others, and the willingness to attend to our communities and physical environment.

This family dynamic is itself influenced by culture and as such is programmed into our unconscious as well as our conscious behaviors. The nurturing role of the mother is so important that it affects the whole digestive tract as well the vagal network that regulates all of our autonomic nervous system.

The function of the mother is to provide for the needs of her children and educate them about the ways of the world. She protects and nurtures the body as well as every aspect of her children's wellbeing. Her job is to support the child in its strengths and to provide education. The mother has to be attuned to the innate ability of her children, as well as to any destructive tendencies they may have, in order to guide them in their early exploration of the world. She is the nurturer, the teacher and the protector. Most early childhood experiences are supervised and guided by a mother, not always the original mother but often a female familiar with the function of mothering.

In this task the mother is greatly assisted by a wonderful talent called empathy. This ability to feel and know without being told—derived from the oneness of the heart—is what supports the mother in fulfilling her role. In addition to providing an inner understanding, empathy also promotes caring, which plays a great role in bonding and in ensuring that the child's needs are met.

Ideally, the mother feels oneness with the child, if she did not she probably would not care and would not be very effective at providing for the child's needs. Because she cares, the mother wants to do the best possible job of building her child's strengths and preparing her or him for life, even if it means serious sacrifices on her part. Mothers have been known to give their lives for their children, demonstrating both the strength of the bond and of the commitment.

Our mother's care is primarily reflected in our psyche in the following ways: self-esteem, self-confidence, sociability and a sense of social inclusiveness. By meeting our need for comfort, the mother communicates that we are worthy to receive. This is reflected in the way we take care of ourselves, the type of relationships we create, and the position we claim for ourselves in the world. Because education largely comes through example, in order to communicate this skill, the mother must be aware of her own needs. She must know how to take care of herself and ask for what she needs.

When the mother provides us with experiences that are challenging but tailored to our ability level, we learn self-confidence and responsibility. This is manifested in the ease with which we approach tasks, the freedom with which we initiate human contact, and the manner in which we receive feedback—as well as our willingness to learn.

By teaching us how to accept and express our needs, desires and aspirations appropriately, we learn how to deal with our emotions and how to create effective and mutually fulfilling social interactions. The mother protects us from accidents and consoles us when we are hurt, teaching us to feel safe and to trust in our environment and in our ability to recover. This provides us with the sense of power necessary to choose our direction and complete our goals. It would be appropriate to say that the mother creates the primary foundation upon which all of our development will rest. It is important to remember that mothering, like all of the other functions of parenting, is ongoing.

The impact of our parents on our psyche may have been more or less beneficial. We need to acknowledge that same process is still taking place in our lives. There is a child consciousness inside of each of us that constantly needs the supportiveness and nurturing of a mother. Even if our mother was deficient in her role, and the internal movement of mothering ourselves is not very strong, we have a responsibility toward the child inside of us to re-create a pattern of inner parenting that is truly caring and supportive.

Emotions are particularly important in relationship to Inner Mothering. The mother needs to teach us how to appropriately express our needs, desires and aspirations. That appropriateness depends upon communication skills. In infancy and early childhood the primary mode of communication is the spontaneous expression of emotions. Through our emotions we communicate to our environment our need for comfort, security, understanding and attention. The fulfillment of these primary needs is paramount in establishing our self-esteem.

As we get older and develop new communication skills, we are encouraged to switch to more socially acceptable modes of expression. However, our emotions are still operating externally as a way to emphasize our messages. In addition, they also operate in the form of inner and outer disturbances to draw our attention to the fact that our basic needs, wants or aspirations are not being fulfilled.

To a large degree the mother is the interpreter of the child's emotions; she combines the information provided by the child's expression, her intuition, and her common sense to address the needs of the child to assure his or her wellbeing. As an adult, the relationship between the mother and child in the Inner Family is still the same, and our attunement to our emotions is critical in recognizing our inner state of balance and in taking responsibility for any imbalances.

The ideal mother is one who is in harmony with her self, knows her own self-worth, trusts her intuition, cherishes the relationship with her children and provides for all their needs in the best possible timing. Of course, this mother does not exist, and even if we tried, we could not live up to this ideal. One of the reasons we cannot is that we are all projecting, in our parenting skills, the limitations in our own inner parenting, which reflect our constitutional tendencies and the way we were parented. Unless we make a conscious effort to transform our internal dynamics, the weaknesses of our parents will be passed on through us to our children.

Our parents were not perfect people. However, blaming them will not do anything to bring our life into greater balance. Many parents were out of balance, dysfunctional or even destructive. It is important that we have the willingness to look at these patterns, accept the past for what it was and create within ourselves a new set of parents that will love us and guide us throughout the rest of our lives.

The most dysfunctional mother would be one who does not feel connected with her child and would be reluctant to touch or relate to her or him in any way. This may be a function of self-absorption, resentment, insecurity, disappointment or memory of parental abuse or neglect. The message the child receives is, "There must be something wrong with me; I am not lovable." Depending upon the temperament of the child, he or she may withdraw, seek approval or seek attention through negative behaviors.

Other, less traumatic but more frequent, patterns the mother may display are over-protectiveness, dysfunctional patterns of fear of rejection and having difficulty differentiating her needs from those of the child. Because of the closeness of the mother-child bond, some degree of these patterns is common. It would be surprising if we had not been affected and may still be affected by one of them. While the presence of any of these mothering limitations may hinder the task of mothering ourselves, they are much less traumatic than the absence of love and caring.

In developing a healthier Inner Mother, it is important to understand what mothering is about—what its function is—and to find clear role models for how to do positive mothering. Authentic mothering is an ongoing process of acknowledging positive qualities and successes as well as recognizing and addressing needs and opportunities for improvement. Unconditional loving, acceptance and compassion are essential positive factors. Complacency, making excuses and getting stuck in what is familiar and comfortable, as tempting as it often is, does not serve anyone and greatly limits the expression of genuine potential.

While the Mother is directly associated with the management of our emotions, we also find her influence in the creative imagination, in our self-image. On the mental level, the effectiveness of our mothering is reflected in our attitudes. On the unconscious level, the negative impact of the mother can be particularly reflected in patterns of rejection, neglect, self-abuse and low self-esteem.

The Father

While the role of the mother is caring, the foundational role of the father is to maintain safety and to train the will beyond instant gratification to purposefulness. I call that function of the brain "directing" because it is through the consistent alignment of the will with higher values and clear objectives that we strengthen our character and positively impact our community. Because our Inner Father leads us on our quest for truth and integrity I call the dynamics Authenticity.

While the function of the father is initially less evident, it is no less important than the role of the mother. The dynamic of the Inner Father is associated with the will—our ability to guide in a direction of upliftment in alignment with our purpose as well as the fulfillment of our goals and aspirations. The Inner Father guides our path upward through all our stages of development, from basic survival to enlightenment. I call these dynamics of human consciousness Authenticity because throughout our evolution we are guided by our values and commitments. Some of the critical qualities involved in that process of leadership are trust, integrity, clarity and tolerance. By aligning our will with the Divine, we discover authentic empowerment. This movement seeks answers to the questions: "Where am I going? What are the values that I stand for in my life?"

We would like the father to be solid like a rock, and to a certain degree his role can be seen that way, as it is associated with inner strength. The father represents the strength that provides security, the steadiness that comes with clarity of purpose, and the flow that trusts the outcome.

In our education the mother is in charge of meeting our needs and teaching us how to do the same; the father's role is to set boundaries, indicate direction and assure the follow-through. He is the driving force that moves us to forfeit pleasure and comfort for the sake of achievements. He places aspiration—the pursuit of our quest for a higher goal—above desires.

The primary role of the father is to train the child's will. Not the willfulness of "my way or else," but the willingness to align with a higher authority and deferring our will when it is appropriate, for example, in situations involving our own wellbeing or that of the family or community. He is also teaching obedience to higher authority.

Because this role can so easily become abusive and totalitarian, the father needs to be motivated by a profound quality of the heart—integrity. Integrity is an inner knowing of the truth that motivates us through our life experiences and gives meaning to all our activities. Integrity helps us differentiate between what is true and what is not true for us. It is the voice of our conscience, operating not out of moralism but from an alignment with the heart. In that sense it is different from our convictions, which represent the certainty of the mind. In the heart we know the whole, and integrity means the respect of that which is whole or holy. When the father is reliable and consistent, and exemplifies integrity, his impact on our consciousness is to promote security.

Our relationship with the mother is somewhat symbiotic, but the father represents the first stranger. His predictability and consistency of behavior strengthen the foundation of trust created by the mother. Through our father we trust or distrust, not just our immediate environment but also ourselves and the world. We learn willpower to pursue what is meaningful for us, and we learn to keep our word. By the clarity of his direction, our father teaches us leadership—the ability to lead our life in a direction of truth and to become an inspiration to other people.

We become what we focus on. This idea delineates the fundamental role of the father's energy. It is through our focus that we determine the outcomes of our life. By encouraging us to steady our will and withstand discomfort in order to pursue what we truly want, the father teaches us about taking control of our destiny. He guides us past the satisfaction of our needs, through the cravings of our desires, to the full expression of our skills, talents and abilities.

Through his example and gentle corrections, the father teaches us leadership. His motives need to be pure, and his movement should be flowing and flexible, but his direction must be steady. Imbalances in the father's leadership function can become cold and rigid. In this case the father insists that his way is the only way, his will the only will. This tends to break the will of the child, teaching subjugation rather than obedience. However, if the will of the child is strong, it may lead to child abuse, constant conflict, and/or rebellious acting out.

While a conflict of wills between the father and the child can be healthy in order to develop our individual identity, a continual battle of wills promotes rebelliousness, aggression and ongoing conflicts between the Inner Father and the Inner Child. This pattern, instead of training the will, discredits the authority of our own inner knowing and promotes stubbornness and a lack of positive creativity.

The father may also demonstrate stagnation, the lack of flow or direction. This may take the form of being entrenched in the past and is typically associated with a fear of movement. In the family it is reflected as heaviness, a lack of stimulation that thwarts change and promotes boredom. This attitude in the father will bring either rebellion on the part of the children or foster in them the same lack of passion and ambition.

Sometimes, the father will be preoccupied or simply be chasing dreams rather than providing any leadership in the family. This pattern has become prevalent in any society where the role of the father is to be at the workplace at the expense of the family. Although this does maintain physical security, it often creates a vacuum in the leadership role of the father. The exclusive focus on material goals at the expense of ideals and spiritual values betrays the true dimension of the father's role and promotes a general distrust of authority. As the popular quote clearly states, "Man does not live by bread alone."

I am not suggesting here that an active professional life and good fathering are mutually exclusive. On the contrary, leadership in the world tends to be an example that is inspiring in the family, as long as both roles are maintained in a harmonious balance.

Creating an effective pattern of self-fathering in our lives implies becoming aware of our own values, selecting clear goals, developing the discipline that leads us in the direction we want to go, and replacing ongoing self-criticism with clear intentions, commitment, encouragement and specific actions.

On the mental level, the negative impact of the father is felt in the rigidity of taking certain positions. On the emotional level, it is associated with fear, terror and panic. In the creative imagination, it is related to the projection of negative outcomes.

The Grandparents

The Inner Grandparents are associated with learning, knowing and wisdom, sometimes called cognitive abilities or cognition, and reflection. The more refined form of learning leads us to wisdom. I call these dynamics Wisdom. The question answered by that quest for knowledge and wisdom is: "How do things work and what is the true meaning of life?" Traditionally, elders were praised for their wisdom. Now we tend to dismiss them or relegate them to an old folks home where their foggy ideas do not have to bother us. Yet, the highest expression of learning is in the wisdom we derive from our life experiences.

In this era where so many people have led lives deprived of profound meaning, generosity, integrity or true expression of self, many older people do not seem to have much wisdom to share. Yet it would be a great mistake to underestimate the value of their reflections. In large or small ways, life teaches and reveals to us who we are. Everyone comes to some form of understanding of what life is about. It is through our life experiences that we discover who we are.

The function of the Grandparents in our consciousness is similar to that of the wise elders in many old traditions, one of reflection awareness and practical reasoning. The grandparents are the ones who are detached enough from the day-to-day challenges to observe, reflect, put things in perspective and understand and identify practical strategies. Because of the wisdom of the elders, their advice was considered precious and they were consulted on any major decision. It is critical to train that function in our consciousness.

One quality that fully supports the dynamics of Wisdom is a zest for knowledge and wanting to derive the most value out of each experience. Part of that learning is derived from what we do and how it turns out. Another aspect is realizing that we will never be able to personally verify everything we are exposed to, so we are willing to learn from the knowledge and experience of others. Beyond this we have to distill our knowledge, integrate it with our values and transform it into lasting wisdom. This is the kind of knowledge that talks to the human experience and transcends generations. Even further, we need to have the openness and willingness to share in a way that empowers others in their process of growth and transformation.

One of the major qualities supporting that function is neutrality. That does not mean lack of interest, caring or withdrawal. Neutrality means impartiality, not taking sides, being less concerned with blaming than with understanding what is going on, and choosing a course of action that restores harmony or ensures survival.

I usually tell my clients that in approaching life there are only two questions that provide most of the value in our investigation of life's challenges and opportunities.

- The first is: "What is going on?"
- The second is: "What can we do about it?"

I am not implying that answering these questions is easy. In fact, sometimes it may take a lifetime of research. But it is to the degree these questions are answered that progress and transformation occur. Questions such as "Who is to blame? Why me? How could they?" do little to generate valuable outcomes.

The role of the grandparents in many families is to act as mediator between the parents and the children. Because they are not directly involved, they perceive more clearly the dynamics of what is taking place and can advise each one about how to handle the situation more effectively. They have more past experience to draw from, are less attached to the ego-protection game of right or wrong, and their advice is usually full of common sense.

Through our awareness, we learn how to extract from our experiences what is precious. In that context, beyond causing serious harm, it matters little what the nature or the result of the experience is, as long as we know how to learn from it.

After attending a self-awareness seminar, one of my sons paid me the highest tribute, stating in a letter that no matter what he did, neither my wife nor I ever blamed him. He noted that our focus was always, "What did you learn from the experience and how could you approach it in a way that would better serve you and be more respectful of others?" When I read his note, I was very touched and I knew that through any parenting challenges, we had managed to instill a deep sense of value and purpose.

Since we frequently tend to be reactive rather than neutral or involved in clear choices—our awareness is not always fully present in what we do. To learn from past experiences, we need to develop the power of reflection. Many older people spend a lot of time looking back at the past. While this may be odd to an observer, it reflects the fact that they are not producing many exciting new experiences. So they are drawing from the past to understand and learn what they failed to assimilate at that time or to enrich their present lives. In the same way, we can look back as often as we care to on past experiences to draw more meaning out of them or to enrich our present life with a quality that we discovered in the past.

In our inner consciousness, the Grandparents serve the purpose of understanding life through the filters of wisdom and experience. They help us make decisions based on proper thinking. They act as a mediator between the concern and protectiveness of the Mother, the authoritarianism of the Father, and the reckless impulsiveness of the Child. When the Grandparents' dynamics are malfunctioning in our consciousness, we recognize it by our tendency to theorize and not act, feelings of not belonging, and the presence of negative judgments regarding things we do. The result is usually confusion, defensiveness and an inability to learn from our life experiences.

The way to reprogram the Inner Grandparents is to spend time in reflection, practicing neutrality and looking at our situation from a place of impartiality. View everything in our life as a learning experience. Regularly ask ourselves: "What are the skills that I learned in that situation? What quality was brought forward in that experience? What skills or qualities could I have used to deal more effectively with that situation?"

The more we leave moral judgment out of our reflections, the more effectively we learn from our experiences and the more quickly we correct the attitudes and behaviors that do not work for us. I am not suggesting that morality is not important. It often is a strong component of mutual trust and self-worth. I am advocating a system of ethics validated through our experience. Claim the privilege to make as many mistakes as it takes to learn, as long as it does not inflict on others.

When I was working at the French Embassy and exploring human development, a friend told me a story I found inspiring and which demonstrated great wisdom. He was being interviewed for a job in human resources management for the Department of Labor. The interview went well and at the end they asked him if he had any special requests. His answer was: "The right to make as many mistakes as needed to learn how to best perform in my new function." He did get the job and became a powerful force of transformation, moving from blame to learning in his department.

On a mental level the Grandparents express our ability to reflect, research and organize. However this can lead to over-mentalizing and aloofness or contempt. On the emotional level the Grandparents bring out positive attitudes towards life but they can also get caught up in attachment to the past. That can bring sadness, grief and regret as well as a sense of isolation or not belonging. In regard to our imagination the Grandparents ground any idealism with practicality but may block possibilities which transcend their experience by focusing on what is merely probable.

The Child

The actions of our mothers, our fathers and our grandparents are the foundation for the freedom of expression of our Inner Child. Let's take a look at the special qualities of creative imagination, self-expression, and contribution which are at the core of the dynamics of the Inner Child. Children operate in a field of imagination that is not restricted by life experience. The focus is on me, what I wish, what I can do, what I desire. Because of this, children are naturally centered on themselves and their desires. There is limited discernment about the impact of their actions, either on themselves, others, or the environment. As a result, the primary drives of the Inner Child are curiosity, exploration, self-gratification and excitement.

Children tend to want to own and rule everything, but they lack the discernment to do so in a harmonious way. The special characteristic of the dynamics of the Inner Child is to use the creative imagination to foster his or her unique expression. Its purpose is exploration and self expression, which naturally leads to valuable contribution. The Inner Child's energy, if not channeled constructively, can be reckless, unlawful, confrontational, challenging and, at the furthest extreme, destructive.

Because of these tendencies the child needs attention, both for protection and validation. Lacking discernment, the child needs all the positive qualities of the mother and the father to learn how to direct his or her energy and needs for expression into self-supporting purposeful activities. The child also needs to learn how things work and how to use them in an effective way. The child often lies and denies the obvious when caught in unwanted behavior. As we grow up, the Inner Child needs to maintain the creative spontaneous expression while learning how to share its unique gifts in support and cooperation with others and society. The keys are freedom of expression supported through authenticity, generosity and cooperation. This then constitutes a solid foundation for personal success and socially valuable contribution.

All societies, religions, cultures and organizations set rules and guidelines to channel the energy of the child into socially acceptable behavior. The child needs boundaries, discipline and corrections. How this is done is a critical factor that either allows that energy to blossom or be repressed and turn destructive.

As difficult as it may be to handle the Inner Child energy and bring that movement of consciousness into harmony with the whole, its purpose is paramount and vital. The Child promotes creativity, innovation and many forms of expression, from creating art to conquering mountains. Repressed, it turns into depression and self-destruction. Left unchecked, it leaves a track of addictions and recklessness and a flurry of unfinished projects, unproductive experiences and immature relationships.

What connects the Child with the heart and the movement of love is freedom and generosity. The child seeks the spontaneous expression of its own uniqueness. In doing this it faces multiple challenges. The first is to learn how to function properly and effectively in its environment. The second is to differentiate between the need for expression of uniqueness and the cravings of the senses. The third is to be willing to learn from mistakes, and the fourth is to realize that uniqueness needs to be expressed within the integrity of the whole in harmony with clear purpose and uplifting values.

The key to retraining this movement of consciousness is honesty. The child tends to prefer illusion to reality and takes refuge in dreams and fantasies whenever the going gets rough. More than anything else, this aspect of the consciousness of the child needs clear feedback rather than the admonishing, lecturing and moralizing that most of us grew up with. We need to reprogram the Mother and the Father of the Inner Family to do their jobs effectively so the Child is surrounded with love, caring, clear feedback and specific goals and boundaries.

It may be hard to understand that, despite our growth and development as adult, part of our consciousness will remain a child throughout our lives. We are, in fact, stuck for the rest of our lives with the same child our parent had to contend with when we were young.

Our responsibility is to help the Inner Child brings forward into the world its unique skills, gifts and talents, as well as to nurture when there is hurt, advise when there is confusion, love no matter what. We must teach the Child how to turn every experience into positive learning.

If we do that, the kid inside of us will remain a kid and will be our greatest source of pleasure and contentment. This precious Child will maintain our spirit—strong, adventurous, daring, spontaneous, and full of life and enthusiasm until our last breath.

The natural expression of the child is associated with the creative imagination because the child lives in a world where desires, fantasies, creativity and spontaneity are closely intermingled. To honor the Child inside of us is to pay tribute to life in its simplicity, creative genius, innocence, naiveté, enchantment, wonderment and regality. The Child is possessed with many beautiful attributes. It is our responsibility not to shatter them through moralism, cynicism, rationalism or any other "isms." If we honor, respect and direct these beautiful qualities of youth within ourselves, we will be amazed at how beautiful life can be and how cooperative and eager-to-please the Child inside of us really is.

In relation to our emotions, the Child's imbalance is reflected primarily through anger, rage, frustration and hate. On the mental level, the negative child expresses through false assumption and deceit. Because of the intense programming that is received in childhood, unfinished business from our childhood is prevalent in our unconscious and often takes the form of unmet expectations, humiliation and rebelliousness.

We have just explored in greater detail the working of the Inner Family with the potential strengths and weaknesses. Now we want to look at the foundation of each of these powerful dynamics of our brain and how we can reprogram any restrictive patterns and expand our personal effectiveness.

Positive Expressions of the Inner Family

The diagram for the Positive Expressions of the Inner Family summarizes much of the material we present in this book. The center circle represents the Inner Peace which resides in the Heart. Just outside of that, in the darker squares, are the foundational attitudes for each member of the Inner Family as they align with the Heart. In the center of each quadrant is the primary focus of that member of the Family. The other qualities listed are additional positive aspects of the dynamic of each member of the Inner Family.

- The Mother supports our relationships to our self, others and the world. The foundational attitude is Respect, leading to a focus on Responsibility.
- The Father supports direction and purpose. Trust in God is the spiritual foundation and Clarity is the essential focus for leadership.
- The Grandparents reflect that life is a learning process. This implies embracing life as an opportunity to learn, we call this Zest. Wisdom reflects the notion that learning is not just mental but rather a process of turning each experience into something transformational that can be shared.
- The Child supports our unique expression. Generosity is essential to go beyond our self importance and Spontaneity is necessary to move beyond social constraints.

Positive Expressions of the
INNER FAMILY

MOTHER		FATHER	
Service	Care of Others	Integrity	Leadership
Responsibility		**Clarity**	
Self-care	Respect	Trust	Tolerance
	INNER PEACE		
Learning from Experience	Zest	Generosity	Authentic Expression
Wisdom		**Spontaneity**	
Teaching	Other Learning	Cooperation	Contribution
GRANDPARENTS		**CHILD**	

© 2016 Babinetics, LLC.

To help you assess how effectively each member of the Inner Family is functioning in your life, you can go to the Appendix on page 219 and answer the questionnaire. Do your best and answer as honestly as possible. If you want a more accurate point of view, ask a trusted friend to answer the questionnaire in terms of how they perceive you in each one of those areas of your consciousness. But do not turn it into a guilt trip. Awareness itself is transformational and what you learn may be enough to initiate profound changes.

A Call to the Mother

—

That she will see me,
nurture me for all that I am.

That she will wrap me in her arms,
shine her radiance upon me.

That she will heal me when I am ailing,
reinforce me when I am well.

That she will weep when I am suffering,
rejoice when I have found joy.

That she will help me to stand when I have fallen,
rest with me when I am weary.

That she will cleanse away my excess,
fertilize my newly-sown seeds.

That she will always believe in me,
encourage me to dream ever-bigger.

That she will stand certain
in the knowing that I will

see her
nurture her
weep for her
rejoice in her
hold her
rest with her
believe in her
heal her
love her

in return.

Chapter Four

THE DYNAMICS
OF THE INNER MOTHER

Between Mother and Child

⁓

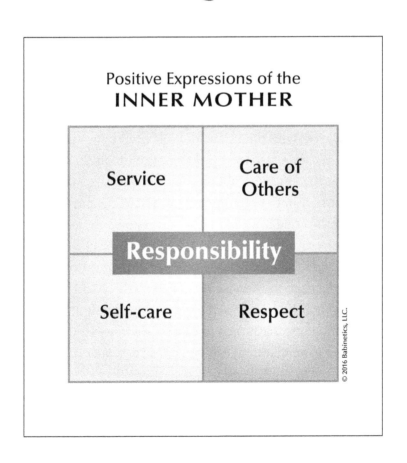

Positive Expressions of the
INNER MOTHER

Service

Care of
Others

Responsibility

Self-care

Respect

© 2016 Babinetics, LLC.

While we are all too aware of the tremendous impact emotions have on our lives, we have not been given many tools to deal with them in an effective way. In this chapter, we will look at the nature of emotions, their dynamics, what happens when they are misused and/or misunderstood and how we can learn to use both negative and positive emotions to our advantage.

The Source of Emotions

The source and purpose of emotions can be elusive for many. We work with them, release them and express them, but what are they? How did they come into awareness? What are they supposed to accomplish?

One day, observing the interaction between a mother and her baby girl, the answer to these questions came to me in an instant. Whenever the child did not feel comfortable, she would cry or squirm or scream to obtain relief. Invariably, the mother would attend to the child until harmony was restored. It became clear that emotions in this sense are simply a form of language: a primitive, yet quite effective form of communication used by children to relay to their mothers and to the world what they need. Because children at birth, and for a long time after, do not have at their disposal words to express their needs and desires, they resort to an instinctive response that describes their state of contentment or displeasure.

Depending on how effective the mother is at interpreting these signs, the child feels more or less competent, understood and safe. In this context, it is easy to understand why women are said to be more intuitive and how much of the child's welfare depends on the mother's intuitive ability.

This form of language does not disappear when we grow older. Words become another way to communicate, yet to a great extent, the emotional response still is how we express our satisfaction or displeasure—more than the words themselves. The primary function of emotions is a call to action toward the fulfillment of perceived unmet needs.

The Nature of Emotions

Understanding the purpose of emotions does not really tell us what emotions are. Again the answer is found by observing young children because, at that age, their spontaneity is intact. Emotional expression is closely related to the body. The satisfaction or deprivation of certain needs triggers an internal mechanism that instantly elicits a physical response in order to convey pleasure or attempt to produce change. Emotions mobilize our energy toward the achievement of goals. Emotions are not the movement itself, which is done by the body; they are the mobilizing of life force that motivates and propels the body into action—an energy charge that disperses itself through activity. This explains the disastrous effect caused by that same energy charge when it is not allowed to disperse. This is also why acupuncture places such a heavy emphasis on the role negative emotions play in the pathology of certain organs.

The Impact of Positive Emotions

Now that we know more clearly what emotions are about, let us examine the impact they have on our lives and how we can transfer them from one situation to another to increase our resourcefulness. It is easy to understand how beneficial positive emotions can be in our lives. They tend to dictate our level of involvement. When we feel good about something, we want to participate in whatever it is that makes us feel that, whether it is a relationship, work or an experience. Positive emotions reflect our level of attraction to something and mobilize energy to support our involvement with what we are attracted to.

Positive emotional states can be recalled to assist us when the going gets rough. By recalling a situation from the past that carried a strong, positive emotional charge, we can access that state within ourselves to assist us in dealing with a present challenge. The following process can help.

Accessing Positive Emotional States Exercise

- Take a situation that bothers you and allow yourself to acknowledge the emotions you are experiencing without judgment.
- Let go of your attachment to being right.
- Ask yourself what quality or feeling would be the most helpful to assist you in resolving the situation you have selected to work with.

- Recall a time in the past when you felt that feeling or demonstrated that quality in a way that produced positive results.
- Reconnect with the feeling you had at that time—as powerfully as you can—and alternate in your mind between the two situations until you experience the resolution of the conflict or achieve a better sense of how to handle it.

This approach is part of what neuro-linguistic programming (NLP) calls reframing and is an effective way of using positive memories to increase our personal empowerment.

There are three elements that can interfere with the effectiveness of this process:

1) Being unwilling to change
2) Not being clear about what quality or skill would be helpful for authentic change
3) Not being able to recall a past situation appropriate to the present need

The first situation requires strategies we will discuss later in the section on how to disperse negative emotions. The second condition often requires a few tries before discovering the right quality or skill. The third is often related to feelings of low self-worth and lack of self-acknowledgment. An indirect way to deal with these situations is to imagine you're someone else, to picture someone else having a quality, or make up an appropriate situation and practice how it would feel to have it yourself, then transfer the feeling to the situation in which you need it. This is called modeling.

One of the reasons the process of transferring an emotional state from one situation to another works so well is that, according to research, only one-fifth of our brain is time-referenced—the rest of the brain does not distinguish between the past, present or future.

Emotions are usually associated with either the limbic or reptilian sections of the brain, neither of which are time-referenced. The left-brain hemisphere, which is strongly time-referenced, often wants to interfere, not comprehending how this process works. Despite this, any quality, strength, or resource you have established in the past is available to you now and for the rest of your life. In fact, life is a series of experiences that awaken resources that were always present within us.

The Impact of Negative Emotions

Let's now consider the impact of negative emotions, their potential value, and how we can use them to our advantage.

Just as positive emotions are key to our involvement in life, negative emotions tend to lead us away from participating fully. Because of the impact our emotions had on our mothers and other primary caretakers, we may use our emotions in an attempt to rule our universe. Using emotions such as anger, fear, guilt and sadness in an attempt to control other people is so prevalent that it can seem to rule human interactions, from family dynamics to world politics. Much of this "power play" is also going on within us among the different members of the Inner Family. This is often the cause of much of our internal confusion and pain. Learning how to use our power well and to the greater advantage of all concerned, internally and externally, is a great talent that few of us have mastered.

Because of the incredible power of emotions and their potential effects, the Chinese referred to the negative emotions of hurt, anger, worry, grief and fear as the "five inner devils." I have extended the list and regrouped them around the major organs of the body linked with the corresponding members of the Inner Family.

Emotional Blocks and How to Deal with Them

One of the difficulties encountered in working with our emotions is that they were designed to assist us in getting what we needed from our environment when we could not communicate in any other way. For some, that produced the expected result and, unless we were properly educated in expressing our needs in others ways, we most likely became little tyrants, manipulating our environment with the emotions that seemed the most effective in childhood. For others, emotions were repressed through physical or emotional abuse, and/or we were asked to justify why we were upset. As a result of these kinds of responses, whether obvious or subtle, we learned to deny or justify our emotions, thus preventing their natural flow. This can create addictive emotional patterns that are difficult to break.

Emotions are a form of energy that releases itself through action. Two major mechanisms are involved in inhibiting the natural expression of emotions: denial and justification.

Denial

The process of denial may be either conscious or unconscious, generally the latter. Usually it carries some level of fear promoted by outside forces such as parents, friends, children, a boss or any kind of authority figure. This fear is the result of a direct threat, memories of threats or punishing actions, or simply an imaginary threat associated with old memories.

When these kinds of emotions are triggered, they may conflict with the image we want to hold of ourselves or want to project. The direct result is that the emotional charge is denied or concealed and strong vital energy is stored in the body producing various negative consequences.

Justification

The second mechanism that blocks the natural movement of emotions is justification. Many people are not aware that by justifying their emotions they are in fact holding internal tension and not allowing the energy to move toward more creative endeavors. When we say "the reason I am angry, frustrated, or afraid is . . .," we have to live with the emotion we are holding onto until we are willing to either take an action that resolves the situation or we change our point of view.

A typical example of this is demonstrated whenever people hold onto something someone did to them in the past. When we blame our emotions on someone else or on external circumstances, we are in the same predicament. By not choosing to take responsibility for our emotional responses, we give our personal power away and end up living in a state of emotional turmoil, often feeling powerless to change.

The Effect of Emotions on the Body

Because emotions were primarily designed to obtain the satisfaction of basic needs, they tend to promote survival actions that require a high degree of energy, like anger or fear, which promote fight or flight. Or they tend to depress our energy as in the cases of worry, guilt, shame or sadness. As a result, their impact on the body is profound. Expressions such as "dying of a broken heart" or "venting one's spleen" clearly reflect that we are aware of a relationship between emotions and the body.

Wilhelm Reich, a student of Freud, emphasized the relationship between repressed emotions and the posture of the body. In his view, the energy of repressed emotions accumulates in the body tissue, forming "body armor." The tension in the muscular tissue prevents natural bodily expression and can dramatically affect people's relationships with themselves and others.

Emotions affect both organs and muscles. Each emotion simultaneously affects a specific group of muscles and organs, and the inhibition of their expression prevents energy from being released, creating multiple energy blocks that can have a profound effect on health.

Emotions and Specific Organs

Typically, each emotion gets stored in a specific organ and muscle group in the body: the heart with hurt, the lungs with sadness, the spleen with worry, the kidneys with fear, and the liver with anger. However, because of circumstantial associations, powerful feelings may be locked into unexpected areas.

Once, I felt something unusual in the big toe of a female client. While I was massaging it with a little bit more attentiveness, she started sobbing with convulsive waves of tears. She told me in a little voice that when she was six years old she had broken her toe at the same time her grandmother was dying in the hospital. She related to me that she felt that the emotion was partially related to the fact that her mother did not have much time to comfort her under the circumstances, but that mostly she was re-experiencing the sadness of the loss of her grandmother. She remembered how much her grandmother had loved her and cared for her. Even though the toe had been healed for a long time, it was still holding a strong emotional charge.

The body stores memories and their emotional content, but sometimes due to certain relationships particular to each individual, the emotions are not localized in their most frequent sites. The chest and lower back are the areas in which issues related to death and grieving are most commonly stored, yet in this case the memory was in the big toe.

Releasing Negative Emotions

Emoting

One of the ways emotions are expressed is through emoting or the sudden release of the pent-up energy, in a way that clearly demonstrates outwardly the state of inner imbalance. This consists in crying when we are sad, withdrawing or running away when we are afraid, and striking, hitting, or yelling when we are angry.

There is nothing necessarily wrong with any of this, and it can be appropriate at times, especially to draw attention from others to powerful internal needs. However, emoting is not always appropriate and often can be quite ineffective. One of the problems with this strategy is that people may respond as intensely as we are emoting, escalating the situation into total chaos or even physical harm. In addition, we can lose control of a situation, lose our job and damage our relationship with others and ourselves. If you have ever observed anyone who has lost control of his or her emotions, you probably saw how ineffective and potentially damaging this could be.

Living in our society requires that, at times, we control our emotions. We cannot hit everyone we get angry at, cry each time we are hurt, or shy away from everything we are afraid of. So, let us look at other ways to release the energy charge caused by repressed or overly controlled emotions.

Catharsis

One strategy very close to emoting is called catharsis. This is the physical expression of the emotion, done in a "safe space" that does not hurt anyone. Many of us naturally discover a place for ourselves where it is safe to let go and release pent-up emotions, such as a private room in our home or when watching an appropriate movie to stimulate the right mood by ourselves. However, people who do not feel safe enough by themselves, or with friends or family, may need the presence of a therapist. Many clients, feel safe and accepted with professional healers and can let go and allow themselves to release.

For catharsis to be effective, certain conditions seem to be optimal. If you are on your own, make sure you are releasing emotion and not building up new levels of tension by talking yourself into greater and greater levels of melodrama. If you are with friends and relatives, make sure their role is clear, that they stand in loving neutrality, neither judging nor lecturing, nor getting so caught up in identifying with your issues that they lose objectivity. What we usually need in order to get beyond our negative emotions is love, clarity, and action. Surround yourselves with people who exhibit these qualities and you will find that you will move more quickly through your unwanted emotions. These people will support you without turning you into an emotional cripple.

Working Out

Another method for releasing emotions, used by many action-oriented people, is focused movement, what some call "working out." This consists of turning emotional energy into physical energy. This way of releasing pent-up emotions can take different forms, from compulsively cleaning up the house when upset at one's spouse to leaving the house in the middle of an argument to walk around the block to cool off. While the process of cooling off adds an element of disengaging from the situation, it also involves a physical activity. Any form of strong physical activity will release unwanted energy or get energy moving, including if the emotion is of a depressive nature. Because depression tends to inhibit movement, the very fact of moving and shifting our posture may have a powerful impact. Research in neuro-linguistic programming has shown that it is very difficult, if possible at all, to stay depressed while looking up and jumping up and down.

This strategy to deal with emotions is often spontaneous and unconscious, yet it is quite effective and can become a way of decreasing one's stress level and improving one's general health. The focus of many corporations on regular exercise for their employees reflects the realization that people who work out regularly are less tense and more effective on the job.

A note of caution: Competitive sports are usually not effective for decreasing emotional stress. They can often produce a great deal of negative emotion both in the performers and the spectators. The best working out strategies are noncompetitive. The more joy they bring, the more effective they are. It is also important not to mix this activity with stress-producing thoughts.

I have seen executives have business conversations while jogging, pedaling exercise bikes in the gym, or lifting weights. I suggest using working out as a complete physical release, where the mind is allowed to let go and relax. It is becoming well established through research that the mind has a direct impact on the level of tension in the body. It is counterproductive to be involved in a stress-reduction activity while also being engaged in producing more stress.

Using Creative Visual Release

Another way of reducing emotional overload, which we often practice without being aware of it, is using the creative imagination.

Dreams, Fantasies, and the Creative Imagination

Research on dreams clearly establishes that dreaming is a necessary function of our psyche and that preventing people from dreaming invariably produces temporary mental disorders. We all have had the experience of working out difficult situations in our dreams, of going to sleep angry or hurt and waking up in a good mood. Dreams often act as outlets for our imbalanced emotional energy. Unfortunately, many of the same repressive influences that limit our emotional release when we are awake also operate in our dreams. This limits the effectiveness of this natural process.

In emotionally loaded situations, another way we cope is through the creation of fantasies, or daydreaming. While the practice is more common when we are younger, fantasies are a common way of letting go of emotional tension. If you observe your thoughts carefully when you enter what you perceive as a dangerous area, you may realize that you are creating various scenarios to prepare yourself for eventualities. This process mobilizes your emotions to prepare you for survival actions. However, whenever you do not feel totally competent to deal with the situation you are creating in your mind, you might give yourself added attributes to cope with your sense of deficiency. You might pretend to suddenly know karate or rehearse something positive you once saw on television. This strategy helps you release the tension you were building inside.

In the same way, when you have not been very effective in a situation, you can go back over it in your creative imagination to balance the level of discomfort you are experiencing. In fact, we sometimes are able to convince ourselves so thoroughly, that when we describe the situation to somebody else, we give a revised version. Sometimes it may be even more effective to imagine being someone or something different from yourself.

If we imagine ourselves running when we are paralyzed with fear, we free up that energy and allow a greater flow of movement in the body. Similarly, if we are angry and imagine having the biggest possible tantrum, the energy of anger disappears. I do not suggest imagining violence. The technique is even more effective when we add an element of humor. Imagine that someone who terrifies you is sitting on the toilet, for example. Create your own humorous fantasies.

The danger is in confusing fantasy and reality. One way to avoid confusing fantasy and reality is to keep your imaging to something that is realistic, not just designed to make you feel good but to truly improve your abilities. Instead of imagining yourself as Superman or Wonder Woman, imagine what quality you would need to address the situation in a way that would be beneficial to all concerned. Then visualize yourself as already having that ability and applying it to the situation. Stay focused on transforming your behavior in alignment with what you truly need. Be creative but stay realistic.

Creative visualization is an attempt at using the imagination to alleviate emotional imbalance and release pent-up emotional energy. The great advantage of this technique is that we can practice it any place and under any circumstances without risking negative social consequences. The drawback is that unless we consciously commit to changing our ineffective behaviors, it may not actually change the disturbing situation.

Whenever we imagine performing a movement, it appears that the same neural activity is involved in the imagining as is involved in the actual body performance of the movement. Emotions mobilize our energy toward action and often these actions are not socially permissible. As we imagine the external movement, it releases the energy charge produced by the emotion and brings the body back to a state of balance, thus also helping us change our behaviors.

"Sitting" in the Emotion

We have looked at various ways to release emotional energy through the body and the creative imagination, and we have noticed that there were advantages and limitations to all these approaches. We can also release emotions by simply staying with them rather than running away from them.

Recall that there are two ways in which we lock emotions inside the body: denial and justification. Both are based on our programming about right and wrong. If we feel that the people or circumstances promoting emotions were wrong, we tend to use justification. If we cannot justify our emotions, we enter into denial. We also tend to use denial if we do not like the emotion we are involved in. Staying or sitting in the emotion is simply allowing our selves to feel the feeling rather than analyzing and judging it. It is recognizing the emotions for what they are: *energy fields designed to prepare us for action.* We do have a responsibility to figure out what is going on and how we could deal with the situation more effectively. And we need to allow the emotion to resolve itself before we can effectively process what is occurring. Try the following exercise for your own experience.

Process for Sitting in the Emotion Exercise

- Imagine that you just had an argument with someone. You are probably upset. Your emotions have been stirred up and many may be involved: anger, fear, hate, frustration, guilt, shame, worry.

- Ask yourself what the dominant feeling is and allow yourself to feel the feeling without any judgment.

- Do the same with each feeling as it comes up.

- Almost always, you will notice eventually that the feeling decreases to a level that is manageable and no longer interferes with your action or thinking process.

- When the emotion is not clearly identifiable, often just feeling the feeling is effective because it requires only that you stay present with the physical sensation associated with the emotion.

- If and when the emotion is clearly identifiable, repeating the name of the emotion is very effective because it focuses the mind and prevents the usual mental chatter associated with unidentified heavy emotional states. For example, you could repeat "fear, fear, fear" (or sadness, etc.) and continue doing this until the charge is dispersed.

This approach does not eliminate the need to understand the situation more clearly along with your emotional response. It does, however, liberate the energy charge so you can address the situation at hand with greater clarity. It is useful to allow ourselves to freely experience our emotions rather than label them as good or bad. If we do judge our emotions, we tend to inhibit them and store them in the body where they can create disturbance and havoc. We will see this approach in greater detail below.

A word about the last step in this exercise, which is to repeat the names of major negative emotions to help disperse the energy we have stored without our conscious awareness: Repeating the names of the negative emotions might at first appear like a reinforcement of them, but experience proves that it frees the bound energy and allows the negativity to disperse. The willingness to try this seemingly nonsensical approach with an emotion with which you are having difficulty, will likely convince you of the efficacy of this method.

Emotions Stored in the Major Organs

Let's look at the major organs and the major emotions that affect them to help us visualize more fully their release when sitting with the emotions.

- The Heart is associated with the emotion of joy. When we close our heart for any reason, we experience hurt. There are four main types of hurt, each associated with the dysfunction of one member of the Inner Family. These emotional reactions can be triggered from our own behavior or through other peoples' actions. The movement of preservation expresses itself through caring and is associated with the Inner Mother. When we experience not being cared for, we feel **rejection**. The movement toward authenticity expresses itself through reliability and corresponds to the Inner Father. When we perceive that we or somebody else are not living up to commitments or expectations, we feel **betrayal**. The movement toward freedom expresses itself through creativity and is associated with the Inner Child. When we realize that something we have planned in our imagination is not taking place as we expected, we feel **disappointment**. The movement toward knowing is associated with the Grandparents and expresses itself through understanding. When events or behaviors do not make sense to us and baffle our ability to comprehend, we are lost and feel **abandonment.**
- The organs associated with the Inner Mother are the stomach and spleen; they react to worry, guilt, envy, discouragement, and despair.

- The organs associated with the Inner Father are the kidney and bladder; they store fear, terror, panic, and despair.
- The organs associated with the Inner Child are the liver and gall bladder; they hold anger, hate, frustration, rage and jealousy.
- The organs associated with the Inner Grandparents are the lung and large intestine; they carry grief, sorrow, and nostalgia.

This list is not exhaustive and there is not an actual name for every emotion. These are the patterns most commonly present in our bodies. All of the feelings are natural to our human experience. The feelings we are not consciously aware of experiencing are probably the ones that are repressed and need to be brought forward.

Process for Bringing Emotions Present

It might be helpful to repeat several times a day the name of the emotions you are not aware of experiencing as a means to bring these emotions more present in your awareness for releasing.

- Find a quiet, safe place and sit or lie down.
- After reviewing the emotions associated with the organs and Inner Family members that we just covered in the previous section, make a list that you can easily have at your disposal. Once you have done that, you can either go down the list one at a time or focus on the emotions that tend to disturb you the most or that you tend to repress.
- Select one and repeat the name of the emotion. For example, "fear, fear, fear, etc. . . ." As you do this, you may experience some disagreeable sensations in your body, e.g., tingling, tightness, dizziness, nausea, heat, cold, etc. These are indications that energy is being mobilized within and being released—not that anything is going wrong. Because of these possible effects, do not do this exercise in circumstances that require a great deal of control.
- If the exercise triggers too much anxiety, you likely have repressed a lot of emotions demanding to be released. You may need the presence of a loving friend or a therapist to allow them to surface and pass through.

- This exercise may induce catharsis at first and may require supervision in some cases. I suggest that, at the beginning, people spend at least one minute on each emotion or until they feel the emotional charge has moved through. This is usually experienced as an easing of tension or a sigh of relief.

Let's move through this exercise again, step by step, to review the whole process:

- Find a quiet, safe place to sit or lie down.
- Use the list of emotions you have created
- Begin repeating the name of one of the emotions for one minute or until it is released.
- Take the next emotion and work it through in the same way. Repeat for each emotion on the list.

If at the beginning, you fall asleep before you are finished with the list, do not be concerned; this is very common. The next day begin where you stopped, until you are finished with the list. Progressively, you will be able to do this exercise more quickly and you will become much more aware of which emotions need to be released.

Verbal Communication

Communicating our emotions verbally can have a profound effect. Almost everyone, when expressing emotions in a challenging situation, is relieved when they have a chance to express their feelings. When our feelings are hurt, it is usually because life or other people are not fulfilling our expectations. It is important to share with people around us how we feel about their behavior. Contrary to what most of us would like to believe, other people generally do not read minds and are not necessarily aware of our needs. We must take responsibility for our preferences, clearly expressing our desires. Clear communication involves taking responsibility for our emotions, being clear about our expectations, expressing ourselves clearly and having respect for the other person's needs and feelings.

Communication also works best when we choose an appropriate time, only involve the people concerned, and we create an atmosphere of mutual safety. Shouting and the use of physical force for self-protection are truly exceptions rather than the rule. They only work effectively when they come from a place of wisdom and not of personal imbalance.

Each time we can remove actions such as blaming, finding fault, and "taking each other's inventory" from our communication, the quality of the communication increases and the chances that it will lead to a creative, satisfactory resolution improves dramatically. Because we do not always have the same needs or share the same points of view as others, communication does not always end in mutual agreement. Often the resolution of a conflict has to be a matter of personal preference and choice; e.g.,

"If this situation does not change, do I still want to be involved in it, and if I do, what attitude do I need to promote within myself in order to accept things as they are and learn the most from what is going on?"

Sublimation

Emotions are just energy. We often use this energy to exercise or do tasks such as cleaning that require a lot of energy. This is a form of sublimation. Turning fear into strength would be a good example of taking something sublimated and converting it into positive energy. Turning hate into a higher form of loving would be another. It takes willingness to use the energy of the emotion to serve a higher purpose. Regular spiritual practices such as meditation, prayers of gratitude, and dedication of oneself to serving others and caring for the planet are a great help in promoting this particular form of sublimation. It seems that as we commit ourselves to uplifting spiritual work, we receive special grace and providence, whereby we are taught how to turn even the most negative states into positive upliftment.

The Meaning of Emotions

When early developmental needs are not properly met in our childhood, imbalances are created in the Inner Family. Many of us spend large portions of our lives attempting to restore balance and experience ourselves as whole.

When we are very young, we have many needs we cannot fulfill by ourselves. We need love, caring, understanding for who we are, security, and attention to our creative expression. At first, these needs have to be met through our external environment, then, slowly, we gain more ability to take care of our needs and more clarity and daring in our own direction, and we discover the power of reflection.

The satisfaction of our basic needs has to eventually be transferred from our outer environment to ourselves. Our family environment was not always as responsive as we needed it to be, sometimes even totally lacked the most basic support. As a result, a typical response is to ignore or deny the depth of our own resourcefulness and continually seek outside ourselves for what we think we so desperately need. This usually manifests as compulsive needs for approval, security, attention, recognition and some form of control. Unfortunately, with this approach, we tend to find what we don't want until we realize that fulfillment has to come first from within. As we change our internal environment by strengthening the aspects of our character and body that are weak, we naturally discover our own inner resourcefulness, and, seemingly miraculously, life reflects this new state by providing us with exactly what we wanted in the first place.

Our emotions are a natural feedback mechanism (a group of signals) that tells us how effectively we are dealing with our lives and point us, very specifically, in more positive directions. Each emotion has its own message and mobilizes the energy we need to promote the necessary change. The positive emotions tell us that we are doing well, and the negative emotions invite us to reflect on what is happening, so we may discover the inner strength needed to bring ourselves back to a state of internal harmony and effectiveness.

When love expresses itself naturally, it is impossible to differentiate the various expressions because they form one continuous integrated movement. It is a state of "isness." This is why it is so difficult to describe health, wellbeing or happiness. When love does not express itself freely, it becomes critical to understand where the movement is inhibited in order to restore the natural harmony. Similarly, we are not usually concerned with our physical organs when we feel good. However, when we feel sick, we want to know where the disorder is taking place so we can act on it and regain health.

Love is a powerful dynamic as it naturally harmonizes. Because it emerges from the very source of our being, it is not looking outward for fulfillment. Love naturally supports the healthy dynamics of each member of the Inner Family. Just as the heart is self-propelled and nurtures the rest of the body, it needs the body to be healthy to sustain and express itself. In the same way, love, which is the initiator and the nurturer, cannot survive in isolation. It fulfills itself in its movement and needs every part of us for its expression. Love that does not express itself dies.

Our emotions are like an alarm system that tells us about imbalances in each domain of our consciousness. We will explore these emotions in great detail in relation to each specific member of the Inner Family.

Challenging Emotions Related to the Inner Mother

The first movement that expresses and sustains love is directly expressed through the function of the Inner Mother, in particular caring and nurturing. Often we confuse this movement with love itself. We explore the dynamics of the Inner Mother first because it is the very foundation of our ability to receive and give love freely. We believe that in order to be loving, we have to be sweet and nice and do everything people tell us to do to make them happy. Of course, this most often does not work. Love only respects love. The way to authentically care for someone is by supporting their beauty and perfection. True nurturing promotes strength, providing the elements necessary to allow growth and development. When the Inner Mother goes out of balance, the following emotions tend to occur: worry, guilt and resentment.

Worry

Not knowing about the future can bring worrying: "Will we have enough?" "Are we doing the right thing?" "Is my child in good hands?" Worrying starts with concern and goes into mentalizing—visualizing and dreading potential negative outcomes—then being terrified by our own internal creation.

What is the meaning of worrying? It means you distrust the foundation you have given your child or you do not trust your support system. The remedy for worrying is to move from concern to caring, i.e., taking care of the situation to the best of your ability then trusting that the best is going to happen. As one of my very good friends has often told me, "Do not be a loser in your own imagination."

One useful practice is to place the situation in the light. Visualize a white light surrounding your children, a spouse, friend, car, your body—whatever you are worrying about. Tell yourself that with that light comes guidance and protection. Some people ask for the protection of God, Christ, the Virgin Mary, their guru, etc. Another practice is to repeat a positive affirmation, such as "I have complete confidence in my ability to deal creatively with any situation that may arise in my life." This occupies the mind and changes the focus from negative to positive.

Worrying is not the exclusive domain of mothers. We worry about what we care about and feel responsible for. If worry were helpful as an expression of caring, that would be fine. However it is never helpful. It is counterproductive, fearful and limiting. Worry does not promote the strength and trust necessary to support a responsible expression. There is nothing meritorious about worrying. It represents an attempt at caring but is self-defeating. The things we care about, including ourselves, need our support not our negative projections.

A friend of mine who was fighting cancer once told me: "I've told only those who are strong enough and care enough to see me healthy." Our thoughts have a power we should not ignore. Being responsible means using that power wisely to support what we love and care about.

Guilt

Another emotion related to the Inner Mother is guilt. We all want to do the best job we are capable of doing. As children, we all wanted to please people around us in order to experience their loving and support. We developed beliefs about what was right and what was wrong. "Right" meant that we received approval. "Wrong" meant that people signaled their discontent—either through punishment, admonition, or withdrawal of affection. As we internalized that process, we re-created the same mechanism internally to keep us on the right track. Whenever we think or get involved in an action that is not congruent with our beliefs, we naturally feel a sort of pang inside of us that reflects this contradiction. Consequently, guilt communicates to our consciousness a discrepancy between our beliefs and our actions or planned actions.

To deal effectively with guilt, we have to consider whether we are still in agreement with the belief that is connected to it. If the belief is no longer in conformity with our experience, we need to change the belief.

Let's say that you have a belief that children should always please their parents. You have just been invited to Hawaii for Thanksgiving with friends. You know how important it is to your parents that you be with them for the yearly family dinner. Your internal beliefs about who comes first, you or your parents, is now being challenged and the thought of missing the family dinner and displeasing your parents is now weighing heavily in your consciousness. You might want to reframe your belief as follows: "I care a lot about my parents who have been very supportive of me, and occasionally I choose to do things that more fully support me, even if this is not what they would prefer." Surprisingly, those who tend to feel the most guilt were not well supported growing up. If we were truly supported for who we were, we would know that love is not dependent on what we do. Guilt is often pathological and reflects a general anxiety about our worthiness.

Consciously changing outdated beliefs may be useful. Our parents were more concerned with implanting their beliefs that they held as true rather than helping us define our own system of values based on our experience. Sometimes we continue to value and respect the beliefs that are triggering guilt. In this case, we are still left with options. The first is to abstain from the action or modify it to conform to the belief. This, in most cases, will restore a sense of natural harmony and self-worth. If it is too late, move to the ultimate challenge: love yourself for who you are not what you do.

Another way to deal with guilt is forgiveness. The word "forgiveness" means to give forth, to go forward, and to let go. Your actions have their own results, so forgiving the action is not of great value. However, forgiving the judgment you have of the action enables you to handle the consequences of your actions without despair. Every one of us will, without doubt, continue to make mistakes. Forgiveness is an act of humility and a statement of trust in the power of love.

Guilt is comparable to a fire alarm. As the alarm detects smoke before the fire has destroyed everything, guilt tells us that there is an imbalance in our consciousness. Although the fire alarm is useful, it does not alter the behavior that caused the fire. In the same manner, guilt is not a substitute for reflection and new commitment. No one would be crazy enough to leave the fire alarm ringing indefinitely to remind them of the possible danger! To the best of their ability, they would learn from their mistakes and go on—whether the house burned down or the alarm detected only a steak overcooking in the oven.

Guilt is a valuable signal, worth listening to, but it does not work as a form of ongoing punishment or to prevent future mistakes. If it did, we would all be perfect beings by now. Love is the most powerful healing and transformative power in the universe. It is a fool's task to attempt to negate its natural healing power by conditioning it. Regardless of your actions, you are worthy of your own loving. As doctors do not prescribe remedies to those who are already healthy, do not wait to be perfect to love yourself.

No matter what you have done in the past or how you may not be living up to your expectations, never give up on yourself. Love is a process—not just the reward. As people know this, they live less in fear and grief over mistakes. If we understood the power of love and forgiveness, we would not be so insistent on being right and we could more easily learn from each other.

Chronic guilt results from perfectionism—the belief that no matter what we have done, it should have been better. Despite the praise that perfectionism receives in many circles, this attitude is basically unhealthy and promotes more pain and suffering than almost anything else. It denies unconditional loving, it denies that life is an ongoing learning process, and it denies our own individual rhythm of growth. Acknowledgment, forgiveness, and daring are what promote excellence—a true upgrade from the devastating results of a standard of perfection. Not feeling that we are good enough or that something about us is not good enough has been strongly correlated with cancer. I have worked with many people with cancer and have found that this trait of lack of self-esteem is frequently a common denominator. It may not be the cause, but it is definitely a component.

Resentment

Like guilt, resentment begins in a belief that our caring should be perfect. Within the family, either the mother could be having trouble with her role or the child could be displeased at how he/she is being cared for. In guilt, the knife is being turned against ourselves; in resentment, we turn it outward.

In resentment, there is also a belief established in a form of perfectionism: "A good mother should ... a good daughter should ... a good husband should ..., etc." Resentment tells us that people, things, or events are not living up to our expectations. Like guilt or other emotions, it reflects a basic need to feel cared for and the need for comfort but with an element of control. I want to be cared for, but my way and yours are in conflict. When we find ourselves being challenged and experiencing resentment there are three choices open to us to resolve the situation. We can decide that our belief is unreasonable and change it. Or we can remove ourselves from the situation if possible. Finally, we can accept the situation and use forgiveness, clear communication and love as tools to attain harmony.

Forgiveness means letting go of judgment and looking toward the desired outcome rather than the past hurt. Clear communication means focusing on the present and clearly expressing our feelings and aspirations. (This is often all it takes to change a situation.

It is amazing how often we insist that, if someone truly loves us, they should be able to read our minds.)

Unconditional loving is the process of focusing on what connects us rather than what separates us. It also means living up to our own standards and not imposing them on others, realizing that in love there is constant transformation. When people feel our love, they are usually much more willing to move away from their rigid positions. In much of his work on counseling, Carl Rogers emphasized what he called "unconditional positive regard." It is a position of total openness in relation to someone else, combined with the conviction that everyone has within them the resources necessary to deal with all the challenges of life. If we extend that notion to ourselves, we could say that unconditional loving is the inner commitment of every member of the Inner Family to approach disturbances with an attitude of openness and the conviction that we have all the resources we need to deal with life's challenges.

We are in charge of our own happiness and choices. We can share our love with others but that gives us no right to try to subjugate them. As we support the strengths in ourselves (and others) with acceptance, compassion and clear direction, resentment progressively disappears and is replaced by strategies where everybody can win. Resentment is one of the hidden costs of perfectionism. Whether it is expressed in a non-constructive manner or internalized, it causes a great deal of distress in ourselves as well as those around us.

Complex Psychological States

We have talked at great length about emotions as they relate to the dynamics of the each of the Inner Family members. However, some states that involve emotions are not clearly related to just one specific Inner Family dynamic, nor are they just emotional. States such as anxiety, stress, apprehension, depression, obsessiveness, shyness, distrust, etc., are fairly complex and involve multiple thought patterns, subliminal images, and emotional reactions that involve all the different members of the Inner Family.

It is advantageous when dealing with these issues to break them down into simpler components. Often when the major emotion has been addressed, the situation becomes manageable and new insight can be gained about how to deal with it.

First, apply the techniques in the section on "Releasing Negative Emotions." Once the emotions have been released, it is easier to focus on the life context and create the changes in behavior or perspective that may be beneficial.

Because so little has been written or taught about how to handle unwanted emotions, we tend to deny them or justify them. The result of both of these approaches is very costly on the body and often creates hurt and separation in our lives. Insights and practices on how to turn them to your advantage will likely help bring more fulfillment in your life.

Often emotions do not reflect what is happening in our life but rather are aspects of the subconscious that are being triggered. When emotions are overwhelming and feel out of proportion with what is happening in our life, we must be aware that most likely we are connecting with old material from past situations in our childhood, genetics, or buried trauma. One way to deal with these is to go back to the energetic of the heart delineated in the first chapter. Access your symbol and connect with the peace. Take it in fully and extend it to the feeling you have been experiencing until it dissolves. If you are aware of the constriction in your body associated with the emotional disturbance, extend the peace and loving to this area until you experience relaxation.

String of Pearls

—

We are meant to achieve,
to feel our greatness,
though not in the way we are
often led to believe.

Arrival, accomplishment,
completion and certainty
dazzle us with the promise of
a settled sureness of being,
markers of something gained,
indelible moments etched in time
that stand our lives upright,
fulfill our lust for meaning—
concepts that become
our greatest hope, promises that
we grasp so tightly that
they transform into the pitfall of
striving for an outcome
never meant to be.

Do not break your heart
in this way.

Suspend your fervent search
for the definitive certification that
proves your worth,
lends proper weight
to your significance,
assures an end to your
righteous, singular quest.

This is not achievement.

Achievement stems from
repeated acts of letting go,
from the choice to
dispel the need for
one sole, pinnacle moment,
to see your life as a string of
essential moments
tied together,
none more precious than another,
each one acting as
the crown jewel,
the very thing
you have been waiting for.

Chapter Five

THE DYNAMICS
OF THE INNER FATHER
Our Will Be Done

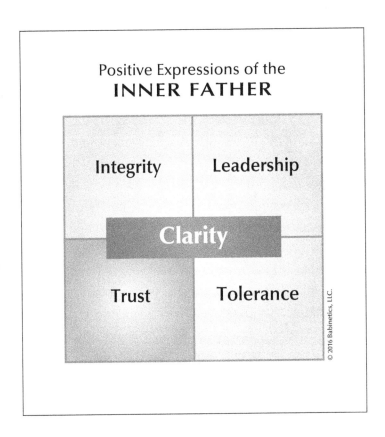

Positive Expressions of the
INNER FATHER

Integrity | Leadership

Clarity

Trust | Tolerance

© 2016 Babinetics, LLC.

In exploring in depth the dynamics of the Inner Father and our search for authentic empowerment, we will understand how to transcend limitation and pursue our own course in life beyond our need to please and seek approval.

The world seems divided between two kinds of people, the ones who follow a precept of "My Will Be Done" and those who follow a direction known as "Thy Will Be Done." The first kind are mostly motivated by their own goals and desires; they tend to be willful and attempt to control whatever they are involved in. The second are more surrendered and tentative, and take the stand that what is happening in their lives is Divine Will. These represent two extremes of same issue.

A great way to understand the function of the will is to see it as a channel between our Spiritual alignment and our service in the world. The two tendencies above exist inside all of us to some degree and both serve a purpose. Man is in the middle as a mediator, or we might say as a channel between Heaven and Earth. Remember the analogy I often use is that of a water hose. To fulfill its function of watering the garden, the hose needs to be connected to the faucet and the water needs to flow. In the same way, our will needs to be connected to the Source and we have to open up to receive the transformational flow of Spiritual love. The biggest restriction to our receiving is judgment. Healing our past traumas and moving to acceptance through forgiveness and learning is essential and we will explore these life opportunities in greater depth.

The ideal, at least according to some beliefs, would be for us to totally surrender to the Divine Will, giving up our willfulness and moving into willingness, a state of total alignment with our destiny and cooperation with truth. Unfortunately, we were not born with an owner's manual that clearly states what our destiny is and how we can best align with it.

In any order, there is an inherent chaos and in any chaos there is an inherent order. The Divine order contains a great deal of chaos or randomness, and it is up to us, through risk-taking, experimentation and learning, to discover what supports us best in our life process. Because we came onto this planet with free will, we have a responsibility to choose and progressively discover the natural order.

The Chinese Taoist tradition expresses this state of ambiguity by describing the world in the form of paradox—everything contains the seed of its opposite. The Tao Te Ching describes this as a state of complementarity: "When all the world understands beauty to be beautiful, then ugliness exists. When all understand goodness to be good, then evil exists. Thus existence suggests non-existence; easy gives rise to difficult; short is derived from long by comparison; low is distinguished from high by position; resonance harmonizes sound; after follows before. Therefore, the sage carries on business without action, and gives his teaching without words."

In the same vein, there is no will without intention and thus willfulness emerges from willingness. It is through the Divine Will that we come into being with our willfulness, and it is through our will that we enter into conflict, misunderstanding, lawlessness and self-destructive behaviors. Yet through that chaos we can learn many qualities such as discernment, strength, caring, compassion, willingness, acceptance and cooperation as we reach greater understanding.

Through our life circumstances all of the lessons that we need are brought forward to allow us to fulfill our destiny. Depending on how willing we are to go through them and bless our opportunities, we either move quickly and relatively effortlessly on our course, or we move slowly and with a great deal of suffering. Who is to judge which way is better? Suffering is also part of the process of discovery and may be exactly the lesson we need in order to move to our next step. So even our resistance is part of the flow and even our chaos is part of the Divine order.

The way we move from fate—which is random and results from choice by default—to the fulfillment of our destiny is through the willingness to make conscious choices and commit to our direction. All through our lives we are presented with challenges designed to bring out the best in us, to mobilize our resourcefulness, talents, and abilities.

Life is a school and, as in any school, we are periodically tested. Testing is not designed to hurt us or to show us how incompetent we are. We are tested at our level of ability and provided with as many chances as we need.

While working for the French Embassy, I reviewed the field of educational technology at a time when programmed learning was fashionable. The most advanced computer application of that approach was designed to provide students with an experience in which new subject matter was presented. Subsequently, a test was administered to check their ability level. If the test was passed, one could move on to the next sequence. If not, the computer analyzed the mistake and referred the students back to previous material to assist them in understanding what they had missed. After reviewing the unit they had failed, the student was again tested to check their knowledge. The willingness to continue the interaction was the only requirement to complete the course. The only way to lose was to refuse to play.

This represents an illustration of how the process of the will and the unconscious mind work together. In both our lives and the computer-assisted learning, we have chosen to be in the course. We have chosen our life because it serves an educational purpose. The purpose may be hidden to us at this time but may reveal itself to us as we go along. The more we resist the "courses" of life, making excuses and blaming others, ourselves, the world, life itself, or even God for having designed such a stupid game, the more painful life gets and the slower is our progress. We have different strategies to resist the process, but they all boil down to trying to change the game rather than play it the way it was designed.

As long as we proceed from the point of view that the game of life is no good or that we can't play, we are pretty much on our own. We may elicit a great deal of pity from other people, but we deny ourselves spiritual assistance. When we courageously face our life as a process specifically designed for us and by us to set us free, we naturally move into alignment and receive tremendous spiritual support.

It can be difficult to hold to that consciousness in the face of adversity. Our natural reaction is to panic, close down, bemoan our fate, and judge our self and/or others for what is happening. None of these strategies changes anything and we are left with the situation as it is. We can either make the best of it or the worst of it. We can choose to accept what is happening, expanding our consciousness and mobilizing our inner resources, or we can contract and add new fears and limitations to our existence.

The ability or willingness to hold a focus is a quality of the will. It is the alignment of our consciousness with a choice. The choice is either positive and expansive or negative and limiting. Some of our choices are conscious, others unconscious. In fact, many choices that appear conscious are hiding unconscious drives and conditioning.

The Inner Family has five major drives that animate the five dynamics and motivate our choices in the world. These drives are natural impulses that promote the various expressions of an Inner Family system. Primary is the need for **love**, the basic need of the human psyche. This instinct toward loving is behind everything else. Other basic needs include the drive for **preservation**, (the Mother), the drive for **authenticity** (the Father), the drive for **wisdom** (the Grandparents), and the drive for **contribution** (the Child).

Everyone is born with a disposition toward one of these directions, a sensitivity that can manifest as strength or weakness; often both simultaneously. The common expression about having the strength of our weaknesses and the weakness of our strengths applies particularly to this domain. Children born with a great sensitivity toward others' needs want to take care of others and make everyone happy. They might overlook their own needs, overextend themselves, and eventually feel underappreciated and resentful. As it is important to not upset peace and harmony, they tend to hold back these negative feelings. This, in the long run might result in chronic conditions of dis-ease, up to and including cancer. I mention the potential impact of what I have just described as it is one of the cancer types discovered by the Simontons, renowned health researchers, who have done extensive work on the psychological context of cancer. Through this, you can see that the great strength of empathy can turn into a source of weakness.

If the five basic drives are well attended to when we are infants and properly directed when we are children and adolescents, we have a solid foundation of loving that naturally enlightens our life choices and assists us in fulfilling our basic drives in a positive, uplifting way. This is an ideal scenario that, unfortunately, does not frequently take place. Many of us have had many of these basic needs neglected, misunderstood, misdirected, or blatantly denied. The most common scenario is that our basic needs were at times attended to and at other times or ways mistreated. As a result, we end up with a mixed bag of conditioned responses resulting in imbalances and challenges.

In order to free our will and rediscover our natural inclination toward health, happiness, abundance and loving, we have to capitalize on everything strong and positive within us and use these assets to heal the past. We need to transmute the traumas, hurt, fear, rage, and misunderstandings that limit our potential and imprison our will by healing the hurt and claiming the wisdom potentially available in our experiences.

The five basic drives of the Inner Family toward love, preservation, authenticity, knowing, and contribution were designed to create a solid foundation within, but any lack in these areas usually results in attempts at getting these needs met outside us. The drive for preservation (Mother) tends to turn into a compulsive need for approval. The drive for authenticity (Father) turns into distrust and a need for control and power. The drive for wisdom (Grandparents) turns into a feeling of being misunderstood accompanied by a compulsive need for recognition. And the drive for contribution (Child) turns into a need for attention and recklessness.

While these needs act as powerful motivators and are the source of our character formation and ego, they tend, when unmet, to perpetrate the feeling of lack, denying us the fulfillment we seek. Instead of providing us with love, which is what we are looking for through the four other drives, we end up with feelings of rejection, abandonment, betrayal, and disappointment. These tend to close our heart and further increase our sense of lack and neediness.

In order to reprogram the past, we must begin with one premise—that we alone are responsible for fulfilling our internal needs. We are responsible for loving ourselves unconditionally and taking care of ourselves. We are responsible for deriving wisdom from all life circumstances. We are responsible for the clarity and wisdom of our choices and the impact they have on ourselves and others. And we are responsible for bringing forward our expression into the world as a commitment of service to the fulfillment of our destiny.

Being responsible does not mean carrying any of these functions as a heavy burden, nor does it mean berating ourselves whenever we don't do a perfect job. Responsibility is a choice to not blame others or ourselves for who we are or what we do. It is a process that simply assesses where we are in relation to where we want to be and continues taking steps that lead us there. It is the willingness to play the game of life to the best of our ability, always going for the next step.

Part of our responsibility is healing the past and re-parenting ourselves. Throughout our lives we have experienced shocks, traumas, unexpected occurrences, and negative conditioning from parents, teachers, ministers, peer groups, our culture and the media. These experiences have resulted in feelings of inadequacy, hurt, confusion, hate, misunderstanding, disappointment, betrayal and many other limiting patterns.

Events are engraved into our consciousness because of the intensity of the impression they have had on our senses. They are words, images, and sensations organized in automatic patterns of response that are locked into the sinews of our consciousness, acting like broken records and limiting our ability to choose freely the direction of our lives. We have reacted to the best of our ability and have created a representational system that involves beliefs, assumptions, attitudes, and emotional and behavioral patterns that are affecting our life. It is the systematic, ongoing programming of ineffective patterns through negative imaging, negative self-talk, self-indulgence and deceit that causes limitations in our daily life. To free our will, we have to release the extra baggage we are carrying so we can travel light and free.

Challenging Emotions Associated with the Dynamics of the Inner Father

Love is sustained through our search for truth and support of our own values. One of our great allies in that pursuit is our will. It enables us to stay on course once we have made a choice and we have committed. Like water, the will is motivated by a single direction that leads it back to its origin. It fulfills itself by flowing. And just like water, it becomes polluted when it becomes stagnant and fixed. When the will is paralyzed by fear, the clarity of purpose is lost, leading to stagnation and rigidity.

The will finds its origin in the will of God's unconditional loving. It fulfills itself in that loving. A key to the sustenance of this flow is recognizing the truth of our own heart and aligning ourselves with that truth in serving God. The temptation in this movement is to adhere to rigid principles, confusing truth with dogmas. Although we are entitled to our convictions, we can easily use them to convict those around us and ourselves, finding fault in everything. As we elevate these convictions by standing in the strength of our loving, we progressively discover a truth that is more elusive.

Love is the beginning and the end, as well as the process in the middle. In that realization we truly fulfill the passage of the Bible that states, "The truth shall set you free." By letting go of our fears we let go of our sense of lack and our territoriality to move into an attunement with the voice of truth within ourselves. This naturally aligns with the will of God and guides us in the fulfillment of our destiny. A good sign of all of this is joy and Inner Peace.

Fear

Fear is one of our most common emotions. We are all familiar with Franklin D. Roosevelt's famous phrase: "The only thing we have to fear is fear itself." Fear is what limits the perception of our true self. Many of us have experienced the grip of uncontrollable fear.

Fear can function in mobilizing all of our resources in facing a life and death situation. Verified accounts of a mother lifting a truck to save her child's life testify to the intensity and tremendous power associated with fear. Fear is associated with the kidneys and bladder. It is not unusual for people to lose control of their bladders when they are facing an imminent danger.

We feel afraid when experiencing our safety as threatened. At this stage of human development it is often not our survival that is at stake but anything we perceive as vital to life or our way of life. It could be our reputation, our personal property, or the people close to us. In some way the integrity of our world appears threatened. Fear is often based on our perception as opposed to reality. Fear is often not in response to something actually happening but, more frequently, to an imaginary situation. This is often triggered by fantasized outcomes, such as when a child is terrified of imagined monsters or we have the fear of making a mistake.

Many of our fears are unreasonable and ungrounded, generated in the imagination. To deal with fear we need to differentiate between what is real and imaginary. When fear corresponds to a real threat, our time to respond is often very short. Fear was created as a survival impulse promoting either fight or flight. The adrenal glands are involved, as the body is being prepared for extreme action or resistance. Anthony Robbins, who has trained thousands of people to walk on hot coals, claims that there is so much hidden power in fear that we need to teach people to tap into its potential for personal empowerment.

This does not mean that fear is always inappropriate. Being afraid of the things that are potentially threatening to our wellbeing may be a precondition to our survival. However, fears do not train us well for life in general. There are often better ways to learn safety and discernment.

We can break through the fear by distinguishing clearly between what truly threatens us and what does not. Further we can become more aware of what we are capable of. This means acknowledging our feelings along with a willingness to focus on and pursue what we want without letting fear rule our behavior. When we truly align our will with spiritual empowerment (the power of love), we become amazed at the degree of ability and resources available to us. One common description of this is a statement made by my Spiritual teacher John-Roger[1]: "The willingness to do brings the ability to do." Notice that it says "willingness" and not "willfulness," which most of the time promotes resistance and interferes with spiritual flow.

---

[1]   John-Roger, Founder of The Movement of Spiritual Awareness, Los Angeles, CA 90051

Dealing with Fear Exercise

You can practice this exercise for dealing with fear.

- Look at an area in your life where you are aware of being ruled by an unreasonable fear. Focus on the situation and allow yourself to experience the fear totally until the tension associated with the fear decreases.
- List the outcomes or the difficulties you are foreseeing.
- Decide what result you really want to achieve and look at how you can achieve it.
- Experience yourself as having all the resources and talents you need in order to achieve the result you desire.
- Commit to go through the experience no matter what happens.
- Imagine how you will feel about yourself after you have conquered your fear. Allow yourself to feel that success right now.
- Take the actions necessary.
- Acknowledge yourself for your courage and your willingness to take charge of your life.
- Look at what situation you want to tackle next.

Here are some recommendations with this exercise: Begin with something that is not too difficult, like making a phone call you have been avoiding. As you gain more confidence, progressively increase the challenges. Never do anything that could endanger your safety or the safety of others. It is important to take small steps in order to build on success. If you do not think you can handle the situation without support, find someone who will stay with you while you do it. Tell her or him how they could support you while you go through the experience.

Fear is a signal that tells us that our sense of territory, familiarity or security is being threatened. It calls for clarity in distinguishing what is going on as well as deciding on the best way to handle it. It often requires the willingness to break through old unconscious beliefs and limitations by mobilizing our will and steadying our focus to achieve the results that will best support us. Every fear we break is a step toward greater freedom. By challenging our fears and apparent limitations, we progressively discover there may be few limits to our possibilities. When we move beyond our fears, we demonstrate our ability to take charge of our life.

Terror and Panic

Different types of fear localize in different areas of the body. The fear of reaching out for what we want in life is centered in the hands. The fear of being seen lands in the eyes. The fear of being caught is in the neck. The fear of falling or losing control is in the legs.

Terror and panic are two emotions closely related to fear that are challenging to differentiate, except they hit us in different parts of our bodies. Terror is centered in the pit of the stomach. This is the main emotional center of the body. Terror threatens us in the core of our being—our potential for action is very limited, and we want to retract into a childlike fetal position to find comfort. From that childlike place in our consciousness, we will attempt to please and seduce to try and mitigate an external force we perceive as insurmountable.

Panic is situated above the heart center, affecting the thymus gland and the heart. Because the heart is so vital, when something takes us by surprise, we naturally want to protect the chest area. Panic suspends the breath, produces palpitations and can even provoke heart attacks. There is usually an element of surprise in the external stimulus when panic is involved. An exception is someone subject to panic attacks. This kind of attack usually starts with a physical syndrome that is surprising, such as a slight asthmatic reaction or chest pain, which can be muscular, allergic in nature or stress-induced. We interpret this sign as life threatening, and the panic is a response to our imagination producing a result we dread.

Panic is usually an attempt to protect ourselves, but it does not produce an effective coping strategy when faced by an external threat. Loud noises, sudden movement and other surprise attacks seem to trigger this response. It is usually followed by the typical fight-flight response.

The strategy to work with either terror or panic is similar to dealing with fear. Allow yourself to feel the feeling without feeding into it. To the best of your ability and without self-judgment, relax and use clear thinking. If the situation warrants, select the best possible course of action and focus all your attention on the outcome you want to obtain. The stronger your focus and determination, the stronger your chance of success.

Remember that whenever fear, terror or panic is experienced, clarity of thinking and focus are critical.

There is another paralyzing fear, which in its most pathological state is called "catatonia." This can manifest as either a collapse of all our strength or as total rigidity from head to toe. It may also be accompanied by shaking. This fear is usually centered in the kidney, bladder, or genital areas—the center of our inner strength. It is usually related to an actual threat and may take place after the situation and real or imagined danger has occurred or when releasing a past traumatic experience. This implies a threat we perceive as beyond our ability to handle. This represents either a collapse or an over-mobilization of energy with no outcome. Compulsive sobbing is often associated with this state. Because this type of reaction is quite traumatic, it is usually a good idea to talk about it, sorting it out with someone you trust.

If, because of any type of fear, terror or panic, you have not acted as appropriately as you would have liked, it is always best to forgive yourself. We are not all built on the same model and each of us has different physiological responses. Some fight, some run, and some collapse or become petrified. Forgive yourself and move back to your self-love. We are not all designed to be heroes or heroines in the same way. As you practice self-leadership and moving beyond fear, you will find your level of security and self-confidence increasing. Your response to external demands will become more and more effective and appropriate.

Healing the Past

Many of the patterns that limit our will and our ability to create the life we want are connected to traumatic events in our life. For this reason healing our past is a critical step in reclaiming our empowerment. Two conditions need to be fulfilled for the release of past trauma: one is the forgiveness of our judgments; the second is the extension of our loving to the part that is still hurt.

Forgiving the Judgment

Much of our conditioning regarding forgiveness has emphasized forgiving others for their actions. In doing so we perpetuate the belief that others are responsible for our pain and suffering. However, others' actions are not the reason we are limited now.

It is our beliefs and attitudes of condemnation that create separation, block our loving and prevent us from moving forward. Forgiving is not a moralistic yardstick of superiority. We can look at the word "forgiving" as meaning "forth-giving," moving forward. Or as "for giving," which indicates we have chosen a life of giving that extends love rather than hate. When another person's behavior upsets us or life does not go our way, forgiving opens the free flow of giving and receiving. As one of my friends puts it, "I am for giving and for getting." When I am willing to let go of negative feelings, thinking, seeing, or doing, I open myself to the grace that is always present. Receiving is a natural outcome of any willingness to give.

Though we may feel morally vindicated—superior and justified—in our judgments, they tend to become bad habits that add to the negativity that surrounds us. Judging our judging is just another level of judging that prevents us from opening our hearts. In addition, judgments usually cause a great deal of pain in the body.

For a long time, I had a nagging pain in my left shoulder, sometimes to greater or lesser degrees, but it was always there. During a workshop on communication I was attending, one exercise required that we move around the room formulating negative judgments about everyone and everything we saw. Within two minutes my left shoulder was in intense, excruciating pain. Every new judgment turned the screw and intensified the pain in my shoulder a little more. Now, whenever I feel the pain in my left shoulder, it is a reminder that I have locked myself up with judgment and it is time for forgiveness. Invariably, when I begin my process of forgiveness, the pain goes away.

It is vital to realize that it is almost never "what" happened, but our judgment of what happened that locks in the ongoing self-inflicted punishment that judgment brings. Judgment is so prevalent in our consciousness that it can pervade our entire perception of the past, present and future as well as impair all our sense organs.

Process to Become Free of Judgment

To assist myself in becoming free of judgment, I developed the list of affirmations below. There are many ways to use affirmations. One way is to use them when you are aware of judgments you are holding; when you experience guilt, shame or self-criticism and second-guessing of something you have said or done; or when you are assessing anything as not good enough. Another way is simply to use the following affirmations at the end of the day to clear your mind of whatever happened during the day and prepare for a peaceful night.

- I forgive all judgments I hold against myself or anyone else, in relation to anything I have seen or not seen, that I am seeing or not seeing, or that I am afraid or want to see or not see.
- I forgive myself for any judgments I hold against myself or anyone else, in relation to anything I have heard or not heard, that I am hearing or not hearing, or that I am afraid or want to hear or not hear.
- I forgive myself for any judgments I hold against myself or anyone else, in relation to anything I have felt or not felt, that I am feeling or not feeling, or that I am afraid or want to feel or not feel.
- I forgive myself for any judgments that I hold against myself or anyone else, in relation to anything I have

said or not said, that I am saying or not saying, or that I am afraid or want to say or not say.

- I forgive myself for any judgments I hold against myself or anyone else, in relation to anything I have done or not done, that I am doing or not doing, or that I am afraid or want to do or not do.
- I forgive myself for any judgments I hold against myself in relation to anything I have smelled or not smelled, that I am smelling or not smelling, or that I am afraid or want to smell or not smell.
- I forgive myself for any judgments I hold against myself or anyone else in relation to anything I've touched or not touched, that I am touching or not touching, and everything I am afraid to or want to touch or not touch.

A shortcut to all of these may be: "I forgive myself for all judgments I hold against myself or anyone else, in relation to anything that I have experienced or not experienced, that I am experiencing or not experiencing, or that I am afraid or want to experience or not experience."

Often when using these affirmations, specific situations come up in our consciousness. When this occurs, it helps to focus the forgiveness on the specific situation and resume the general affirmations.

For example, once when writing the affirmation on forgiving the judgment I had in relation to what I had done, what came to my mind was my experience in England at age 16 when I participated in stealing some music. As that came up, I switched the affirmation I was using to: "I forgive myself for any judgments I am holding against myself or my friends in relation to the music that I stole when I was 16."

When I was focusing on smelling, passing gas in public came to my mind, so I used an affirmation for that purpose: "I forgive the judgments I hold against myself or anyone else in relation to passing gas in public."

When I was focusing on touching, what came to my mind was lust and masturbation, so I used an affirmation to that effect: "I forgive the judgments I hold against myself or anyone else in relation to masturbation and sexual activities involving touching myself or someone else's private parts."

The more specific we get, the more effective forgiveness is. Although summing up everything under "experiencing" may be an effective shortcut, sometimes it does not bring as much material to the surface as when we deal with each sense activity separately. Repeating the series of above affirmations often increases the acuity of our sense organs and alleviates much physical pain and discomfort. In addition, it can bring to the surface many situations in which we still hold judgments against others or ourselves, assisting us in getting free of past conditioning and self-imposed limitations.

Forgiveness has nothing to do with condoning or excusing destructive behaviors. There is no excuse for abuse of power in any form, whether it is religious, political or sexual, or involves murder, child abuse or self-abuse. There may be attenuating circumstances for the people involved in them, but the actions remain destructive and abhorrent. Forgiveness is not a process of justifying the unjustifiable; it is simply a choice to move forward and allow the loving to be restored within our own consciousness, so that acceptance, healing and reprogramming can take place. A prerequisite for keeping the heart open is letting go of judgments, and that is exactly what forgiveness is all about.

Tending the Hurt

Forgiveness is the first step in taking responsibility, recognizing that no matter what happened in the past, we need to provide the healing. Any disturbance in our life is the result of ineffectiveness in the Inner Family. This may be due to tendencies we are born with, our experiences in the womb, conditions of the birth, dynamics of the family in which we grew up or environmental circumstances during our childhood or adolescence. Usually it is the combination of all of these.

Some birth traumas are related to the birth process, such as a difficult labor, the use of forceps or other instruments, breech birth, choking on the umbilical cord or cutting of the cord prematurely before breathing has established itself spontaneously. Others are connected with the environment of the birth, such as loud noise, being slapped on the behind or extremely bright lights. Even more are related to coming to the planet and not wanting to be here. Many people who are not happy in their life and do not support themselves well in the world began their resistance to the process of living at birth.

The best way to retrain ourselves is to effectively parent the child inside of us. It starts with loving. One definition of the process of healing is the application of loving to the place that hurts. To heal the past and free our will, we need to bring a great deal of loving to the parts that have been hurt. These parts are usually revealed through our life circumstances. As long as these places of hurt and misunderstanding have not been tended to, events in our lives will bring them to the surface. If we consciously choose to attend to our own upsets instead of blaming others and insisting on reparation and separation, we are on the track of making ourselves whole.

An upset that stems from an unconscious block is often identified when we cannot find anything that connects the disturbance we are experiencing with our life circumstances or when our level of disturbance is totally out of proportion with the triggering event.

Process for Releasing Unconscious Blocks

An effective strategy when one of these buried memories surfaces is to personify it by giving it an age. You can try the following.

- Check internally and ask yourself: "How old do I feel right now?"

- When you have determined the approximate age, reflect on whether there was an event at that age that may relate to what you are currently experiencing.
- Explore that period of your life.
- Reflect on how you would have liked to have been treated or parented at that time. How would you like to have had loving demonstrated to you when you were that age? Would you have wanted to be held, listened to, counseled or advised as to what the consequences of your actions could be?
- What tone of voice, what attitudes, what gestures, would have been effective to deal with the situation in a loving, balanced way?
- Take your time to check internally and create the perfect scenario for your healing process.
- Once you have done this, close your eyes, imagine the safest place you know and attend to yourself in the way you would want to have been parented or cared for in that situation.

The more precision, depth and detail you can bring to this process, the greater the depth of healing and completion will be available.

The places inside of us that hurt are our "lost children." Treat these places with the same attention and caring you would your own children. They are our prodigal sons and daughters, and we have to prepare a feast for their return. When they show up, tattered and torn, hurt or enraged, attend to them with all the loving they deserve. If you approach hurts from the past this way, there will be empathy for the upset while the loving will sustain a state of Inner Peace. You will then be able to attend to the hurt effectively. By not making the love bigger, people either act in collusion with the abusers of the past or identify with the hurt so much that they experience impotence, rage, depression, etc., all over again (and again and again!). Your past is your past. It only impacts your present when you attempt to live in the past. Let go and move on. If something acts as a trigger and the past shows its face of hurt and reactivity, tend to the hurt with great compassion for that aspect of yourself.

In many cases the healing scenario of attending to the hurt has to be repeated several times before the healing is complete and the strength and vitality have been reintegrated in your consciousness. When you discover one of these "lost children" within yourself, commit to repeating the healing process once a day for at least a month.

When dealing with major traumas, repeating the process of inner loving consistently for one month demonstrates a deep level of caring for the part that has been hurt. Then, as we come across minor upsets from the past that surface as a result of events in our everyday lives, we can attend to them on the spot or set aside a private time to do it later. If we need to postpone the healing, we must honor that commitment at a later time. Honesty is the foundation of trust. By not honoring the commitment to the Inner Child to complete the healing, we damage the foundation of trust in the Inner Family.

Occasionally, upsets are so big and the love has shrunk so much, that we cannot do this on our own. It is then critical to find help. Therapy or counseling centered primarily around learning loving can help you move into caring for yourself effectively. The process is the same, but you may need assistance in restoring natural alignment. If you start the process and it initially seems to be getting worse or going nowhere, instead of better, do not panic or postpone the healing of the hurt; rather, get the help you need to restore balance and harmony.

Good therapy is designed to help you retrain the natural inner functions of parenting that exist in everyone and that are designed to support us and direct us in our life experience. Once we have re-created a healthy Inner Family, we have built within ourselves a natural process of ongoing inner counseling. For some who were subjected to intense and/or repeated abuse, the process may take much longer and necessitate a long-term relationship with a trained professional or ongoing participation in a specialized support group. For most, this process can be a relatively enjoyable process of learning, exploration and completion.

Sometimes, equilibrium might be disturbed by dramatic life circumstances, stretching the inner parenting resources to the limit. Seeking help at that time is a wise choice that reflects a positive drive for self-care. At these times, it is important to view the situation as a challenge requiring external support rather than a failure on your part.

Process for Dealing with Trauma in the Womb

Disturbances often originate in the womb and become one of the unconscious blocks. They could be:

1. Biochemical in nature, e.g., reactions to drugs, caffeine, alcohol or nicotine
2. Traumatic, resulting from an accident in which the mother was involved
3. Emotional, reflecting the difficulties the mother was experiencing with pregnancy or her life circumstances.

The following exercise can assist with dealing with trauma in the womb.

- Whether you are a man or a woman, imagine yourself being pregnant with yourself and attending to yourself in the most perfect way you can imagine. Refer to the steps in the Process for Releasing Unconscious Blocks for generating specific details. (You may want to go back to page 76 to review the process before clearing issues in utero.)
- Imagine being both the mother and the fetus in the womb.
- If you are a man, this process will help you connect with your feminine qualities and gain empathy for

the beautiful, delicate and challenging process of pregnancy.

- If you are a woman without children, this process will help you understand and/or prepare for that role should you ever choose it.

- If you are a woman who has already been pregnant, it will be an opportunity for validation and/or forgiveness. You might now realize things you could have done that you did not know about when pregnant. This can be a tremendous opportunity for self-healing and loving. It is frequently difficult for pregnant women to communicate any hurt or confusion they may be experiencing. They feel that they "should" be so happy, and yet they are going through major changes that are as intense as puberty. These changes often bring to the surface material from the unconscious. Pregnancy is often a time to do a great deal of healing within us. It is also a time when it is imperative to have a good support system. It is essential to realize how connected the fetus and the mother are and how much impact the mental and emotional state of the expectant woman can have on the baby.

- I recommend that you also reimagine your birth, experiencing it the way you would most want it.

- I suggest doing this both from the awareness of you birthing yourself and from the experience of being the newborn. Allow yourself to experience it from within, not as if you were witnessing the birth.

The connection of the mother and child during pregnancy and birth is so symbiotic that re-experiencing both roles in a positive uplifting way may be critical in releasing trauma. If this process seems overwhelming, I strongly suggest you seek the assistance of someone well qualified in rebirthing or bioenergetics modalities to assist going through the process in a safe way.

Adolescence

Adolescence, with its emphasis on separating from the control of the parents and experimenting with every aspect of life, often leaves profound scars in our consciousness. This is a time when we may give up our integrity in order to fit into our peer group, at great cost to our self-esteem. This can then become imprinted in our psyche. Adolescence, with its profound challenges, typically produces well over half the unconscious trauma and incompletion we carry with us.

Adolescence is a time of great change on organic and glandular levels. Physical appearance is shifting constantly, and sexual desires intensify as sexual identity defines itself. It is often accompanied by a tremendous sense of excitement and empowerment, but also with deep feelings of rejection, abandonment, betrayal and disappointment. We often discover our parents are not who we thought they were and that adults often do not have the level of wisdom or integrity we imagined. Idealism and disillusionment often appear simultaneously.

Intense conflicts often emerge in our close environments of family and friends, resulting in deep feelings of misunderstanding and separation. Most children in this time period would benefit from a positive counseling experience, either on a one-to-one basis or as part of a group process. They have a strong need to be accepted as they are, be allowed to define their own values, and be told it is fine to explore and challenge, but that it is not okay to abuse themselves or others. This last message is usually better received when it is communicated by someone the same age or a trusted adult.

For many of us, this external support system was not present, and we went through it on our own. As a result, we often buried many of our feelings and got involved in experimental situations that we later regarded with shame, rage, cynicism and condemnation. In healing traumas from adolescence and reprogramming negative conditioning from that period, the keys are forgiveness and total acceptance of the adolescent years as a time of exploration and self-definition.

What we did during adolescence is far less important than what we can learn from it. It can take many years to get the true meaning and value of specific experiences. Sometimes we have to go all the way in one direction before we realize we need to turn around. The greatest value of an experience may be that it gets us to the point of realization that our approach to life is not working and we need to change our ways.

Ideally, effective parenting in a healthy family has been progressively internalized and by the time the child seeks his/her independence, the foundation of inner parenting is well established. Parents progressively relinquish their role as protector and guardian as the child's ability to make discerning choices and take responsibility for their own decisions becomes more clearly established.

The brain completes its development in the early twenties. Until we are age 25, the frontal cortex, responsible for long-term planning and the relationship of cause and effect, is not fully developed. Adolescent and young adults often lack the ability to make clear choices that fully support them in creating the best life opportunities. As a result, parents still play a big role at a time when young adults think that they should be left alone. One approach that may work (especially if trust is established) is to ask them the purpose of what they are doing and what value it serves for them, others and the planet. We can try to limit the damage, understanding that like us, much of their learning will come from their mistakes.

As we approach adolescence, the role of the mother and father needs to change from that of parenting to one of friend, counselor or mentor, moving more and more toward mutual respect, trust and appreciation. This is a gradual process that requires readiness and practice on both sides.

Unfortunately, things do not happen this way very often. Parents get attached to their role as controller of their children's destiny, often forgetting they went through the same process with their own parents. They try to impose on their children what they call their "experience," which often does not amount to much more than their own prejudices, outdated traditions, fears and inhibitions. Often they refuse to acknowledge that much of what they learned from their own life experience may have little to do with what their children are facing at this time. This challenge is being exacerbated by the exponential speed of continuous change going on at this time.

Children, in turn, frequently tend to assume that their parents owe them everything and nothing should be required in return. Interestingly, this assumption often flows from being overprotected when they were young. They were spoiled, and now everyone pays the price. Parents often are trying at the last minute to correct the mistakes made along the way. This approach does not work too well. Last-minute authoritarian parenting does not repair the damage of years of indulgence. Children need to learn when they are young that giving and receiving are part of the natural order of life, and that gratitude provides much more happiness in life than greed, demands and defiance.

Beyond forgiving ourselves for whatever judgments we are still holding in relation to our adolescence, we need to attend to the hurt through loving, compassion and understanding. When we discover one of our "lost children" still caught up in adolescence, we need to attend to him/her in the same manner we did with blocks from earlier years. We need to remember the need may be different, and this place inside of us may need a different type of intervention, one more appropriate to the specific needs of the time. If you imagine yourself back in that time and apply acceptance and loving, you will naturally move to a place of the respect, support and understanding you needed at that time. You can imagine a context of trust between the parent(s) and the hurt adolescent within yourself, attending to his/her needs with less rigidity and greater equality, and with honest, respectful sharing of feelings and information.

Additionally, we need to examine patterns of defiance, stubbornness, dependency, cynicism, deceit, laziness, egotism, etc., and begin shifting our attitudes and behaviors toward loving, cooperation, respect, consideration, courage, willingness to learn, participation and involvement. It is important in order for healing to take place to look at the position of the adolescent with honesty and realize that our hurt might possibly have been the result of our own behavior, insensitivity, egotism and unwillingness to cooperate with what might have been for our highest good. Forgiveness for ourselves—as well as for our parents and anyone else involved—is in order as well as a willingness to let go of ineffective patterns of behavior we adopted during our adolescence.

Adulthood

Limitation and contraction may also be connected with situations that occur later on in life, often relating to actions we were involved in that did not reflect our inner values. These are often done out of fear or laziness and buried inside so we do not have to think about them. They come back periodically to haunt us in the form of psychological disturbances or in the form of bodily pain and illness.

The most frequent causes involve broken promises, including unfaithfulness, sexual misconduct, backstabbing, unethical conduct on the job and addictive patterns. As we become more aware of these situations, we need to forgive ourselves for our judgments, repair any damage when possible and learn from the past by redirecting our thoughts and actions in alignment with our integrity.

Traumatic and unexpected events in our life come up periodically, often bringing to the surface a great deal of hurt from the past. Among these are separation, divorce, loss of a loved one, accidents, serious diseases, loss of a job, undesired change of geographical location and loss of important possessions. While these major disturbances are associated with serious consequences and tragedy, they can be turned into opportunities to clear up unresolved situations, fears and misunderstandings that were dormant in our unconscious. Remembering to approach these periods of hardship with self-acceptance, forgiveness and a strong commitment to loving can enable us to deal with challenging occurrences more effectively and with minimal amounts of new scarring.

The healing of memories through forgiveness and loving is an ongoing process. As new material is brought into our consciousness by life situations, we have an opportunity to become more and more free of past conditioning. We can become progressively more skillful at determining the orderly, loving direction of our lives in ways that uplift us and provide a source of inspiration for those around us.

A Complete Memoir

—

There is no part
of our lives
that should be
ignored
forgotten
labeled as unimportant —

not the good dreams
the bad dreams
the moments of pure joy
of abject fear
of inconsolable grief —
the swirls of confusion
explosions of inspiration
complete loss of reason —
the realization of
things long forgotten
true love discovered
stories that have become
the hollow bones of our actions —
conversations with God
mother father sister brother
our soul self
renewed self —
the wise eyes of a stranger
geese crossing the road
lilies pushing through snow
the sound of sirens
underscoring questions
of a weary soul —

life is not just one of these
but all of them
strung together
crossing gaps and chasms
finding their way
onto the infinite pages
of your memoir.

Chapter Six

THE DYNAMICS OF
THE INNER GRANDPARENTS

Loving to Learn

∼

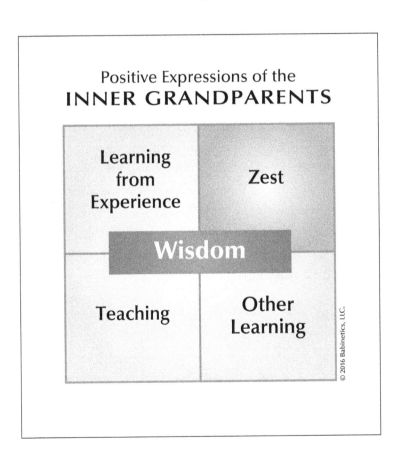

Positive Expressions of the
INNER GRANDPARENTS

Learning from Experience

Zest

Wisdom

Teaching

Other Learning

© 2016 Babinetics, LLC.

In this chapter we will look at the fundamental importance of learning in our lives, what tends to block our learning process and what can be done to enhance our ability to grow and learn.

Before we go any further, I want to make it clear that when I talk about learning here, I am not talking about education in the traditional sense. I am not excluding that aspect of our life experience or minimizing it; I just see it as a small part of a big whole called Life. At every step in our lives, from cradle to the grave, we are involved in the process of learning.

In our metaphorical Inner Family, we saw that learning was more primarily related to the role of the Grandparents or in the Chinese medicine tradition, with the element Metal. This does not mean that learning is the privilege of the old; learning is an ongoing process. The analogy to the Grandparents or elders relates to the fact that our most valuable learning promotes wisdom. However, as the Chinese analogy with metal reveals, wisdom exists in the depth of our experience; to bring it out, we need to dig for it, extract it and refine it. Short of this, we accumulate much experience and possibly a great deal of knowledge—but most probably little wisdom.

Older people who have lived their lives to the fullest are valued both for their knowledge and their wisdom. However, because of the extreme rate of change in our society, their relevant knowledge fades away rapidly while their wisdom remains unchanged. Because there is so much emphasis in our society on the acquisition of knowledge as a tool for survival, we have not paid much attention to how we can grow in wisdom. As a result, many of our senior citizens feel profoundly disconnected as they grow older, since their knowledge is obsolete and they do not realize the potential of their wisdom.

I became aware of this in my relationship with my father, a man of great knowledge and profound insight. As he grew older, much of the information he shared with us and many of the numerous skills he had acquired during his rich and extended life were antiquated, but the measure of his wisdom only increased and refined with age and even his death was, and remains, a poignant testimony to the infinite quality of his being.

It is clear that a large part of our learning is not in educational institutions. It is a lifelong process that starts at birth and some would argue in utero. Studies in early childhood development such as Daniel Stern's *The First Relationship: Infant and Mother* describe in great detail the profound learning of the infant through the interaction with its mother and how this creates the foundation for future social interaction.[2] While this type of learning is primarily instinctive, it is no less significant in our development.

In the book *The First Three Years of Life,* Burton L. White emphasizes the many different forms of learning involved in early childhood development, how interrelated they all are, and how fundamental loving, caring, directing and creative expression are in fostering that process.[3] Unfortunately in most industrialized societies, as we get older the emphasis moves toward cognitive learning at the

---

[2] Stern, D. *The First Relationship: Infant and Mother.* Cambridge, Mass.: Harvard University Press, 1977

[3] White, B. T. *The First Three Years of Life,* Englewood Cliffs, New Jersey: Prentice Hall, 1976

expense of our other abilities. There is no doubt that to function in societies like ours a great deal of data has to be absorbed and many basic cognitive skills need to be mastered, yet to be a fully functioning human capable of loving, caring, originality and leadership, a lot more needs to be brought forward.

Recent works on brain research by Dr. Paul D. McLean, *The Triune Brain in Evolution;*[4]. Howard Gardner, *Frames Of Mind;*[5] and the ongoing research of Dr. Elaine De Beauport[6] emphasize the existence of many forms of intelligence that all need effective training throughout our lives. De Beauport borrowed the concept of multiple intelligences from Gardner and integrated it with the McLean's work and came up with Twelve Intelligences, which she organized in the following manner:

- Old Brain (Primal or Reptilian intelligences) subdivided into: pattern, routine, ritual intelligences and imitative intelligences
- Limbic Brain (Mammalian or Feeling intelligences) subdivided into: affect, emotional, motivational and mood intelligences.

---

4   McLean, Paul. Dr. Paul D. McLean, *The Triune Brain in Evolution*. Role in Paleocerebral Functions. Plenum, New York, 1960

5   Gardner, Howard. Frames of Mind: The Theory of Multiple Intelligences. New York: Basic Books, 1983. Gardner describes linguistic intelligence, musical intelligence, logical mathematical intelligence, spatial intelligence, bodily kinesthetic intelligence and personal intelligence.

6   De Beauport, Elaine, director and founder of the Mead Institute for Human Development. Unpublished research. De Beauport describes the reptilian brain as having ritual and imitative intelligences; the limbic brain as having affectional, motivational and mood intelligences; the neo-cortex left side as having rational intelligence; and the neo-cortex right side as having associative, visual and intuitive intelligences.

- Neo-Cortex (New Brain intelligences) divided into the left brain hemisphere, containing rational intelligence, and the right brain hemisphere containing: associative, visual and intuitional intelligences·

I personally believe that mobilization of all of these intelligences is needed to receive the most value from our life experience.

If I apply the concept of Yin and Yang to the process of education, I see two types of learning, one internal and the other external. The Yang—external or functional—learning is that which is generally addressed in our educational system. The Yin— internal learning—is produced by the revelation and mobilization of inner qualities in response to the demands and challenges of our external and internal environment. As we have all experienced, different situations call for different qualities such as strength, patience, discernment, precision, humor, tenderness and gentleness, and often a combination of many qualities rather than a single one. The mobilization of these latent qualities and talents is the material from which wisdom emerges. Traditionally, this aspect of learning has been somewhat taken for granted and is usually addressed only if the quality brought forward is socially unacceptable for the context and it affects our behavior and performance in a serious way.

New techniques of human development that stress the need for affective as well as cognitive learning affirm that all the qualitative resources we will ever need are already within us in a more or less latent state. All they need in order to be revealed is the appropriate challenge combined with acknowledgment. Even in the absence of positive reinforcement, life mobilizes these qualities, often whether we like it or not, and proper reflection can enable us to acknowledge, in retrospect, the potential wisdom to be derived from challenging or traumatic situations.

The Yang aspect of learning is related more directly to doing than being; it involves a combination of skills and information, e.g., learning languages or physics. Because we cannot always construct a proper context for learning, these are often taught in a more theoretical and abstract manner.

Schools and universities have, for the most part, been designed to provide us with basic social and advanced cognitive skills. Yet generally they fail to teach us how to learn from life itself. The emphasis is on social integration to our peer group and traditional learning styles. They fail to cultivate most of our basic human abilities because they focus on books as the main source of information, tending to devalue our own experience as a primary source of learning and thereby disconnecting us from most of our sensory apparatus.

I have a great appreciation for the new type of learning promoted through the Human Potential Movement, the extension of the humanistic psychotherapeutic tradition presented in the form of workshops designed for the general public to assist people in becoming more aware and developing inner resources. I particularly value the fact that the majority of these transformational seminars focus primarily on direct experience in areas that have been mostly neglected by traditional centers of learning. Many of these educational experiences facilitate the development of the intelligences from the reptilian, mammalian and right side of the brain, and they train us to function with the totality of our brain potential. I believe that by providing a safe environment for our internal exploration, we can increase our ability to extract the maximum learning from our ongoing life experience.

Both the acquisition of wisdom and knowledge are greatly affected by four variables that seem to condition the mental process: positions, beliefs, attitudes and assumptions. We will now examine each one of these, looking at how they can work for us or against us and what we can do about it.

Positions

Due to the circumstances of our lives, most of us develop certain stands or positions we associate with survival. Unwillingness to trust is often characteristic of these positions. The unwillingness to trust can be directed at people by gender, race, occupation, religion, sexuality or through experiences of intimacy, marriage, partnership, children, spirituality, learning, business, politics, wealth, health, poverty, power.

Many of these positions could be classified as some form of prejudice and they promote a great deal of inflexibility. The distrust, terror or panic is not necessarily directed at others. What differentiates those beliefs from other beliefs is that the will is locked into them with no apparent ability or willingness to move to a more flexible course regardless of how damaging the position can be to us and others. Suicide is an extreme example of this way of being, as are many of the militant and radical approaches to life.

Negative positions block our ability to learn by preventing us from being open to new situations. These positions are often recognizable by the degree of belligerence and irrationality with which we defend them when they are being questioned. When we are so locked up into a conviction we are unwilling to explore another way or another point of view, there is a good chance that a position is blocking our ability to learn.

Because we are so totally identified with our positions, they seem obvious to us. Consequently, we may be unconscious of the pattern that is running us despite its destructive nature. The first step in ascertaining our own positions is to watch with awareness for our dead spots, the areas of our psyche we are unwilling to challenge. Whenever we are convinced of being right and become antagonistic, we may want to look at whether our point of view is locked into a position that is blocking us from entering into new experiences.

Not all positions we take are negative. A stand we take may be well informed and support us in many ways; yet, it is to our advantage to keep an open mind and open heart when we are faced with new situations and people that bring forward strong defensive reactions. At these times, if we can substitute awareness and a willingness to learn from our rigidity and fear, our lives will be profoundly enriched.

Another factor that makes positions difficult to challenge is they tend to be self-fulfilling. When we approach any situation with a locked point of view, we tend to look for evidence that confirms our suspicion, and in this we can reaffirm that we were right all along and nothing has changed.

When I worked for the French Embassy, I had a colleague who hated a certain cafeteria where a group of us frequently met for lunch. When we chose to go there, he would always go his own way, each time telling us how awful that place was and how he could not understand why we insisted on going there. One day, to our surprise, he accepted our invitation to come there with us. We were curious but did not say anything. When we arrived at the cafeteria, we soon realized that nothing had changed. His apparent flexibility was simply an attempt to prove to us we were wrong. First, he denigrated everything we chose for lunch, then he proceeded to select the worst possible dish on the menu—a hot dog with cabbage and American cheese melted on top—a very unlikely treat for a Frenchman. Then he spent the rest of the meal proving to us how right he was about the place and what horrible taste we all had. Positions tend to be like that—we are so caught up in righteousness, we can easily reaffirm them even when we are pretending to be open-minded.

Beliefs

Beliefs are either derived from a certain interpretation of past experiences or are learned in our environment. If we could watch our beliefs, we would be amazed by their subtleness and intricacies. One way to explore this is to start becoming aware of our self-talk.

Contrary to what most people think, talking to ourselves is not the privilege of the crazed and lonely old folks; we all do it most of the time. The fact that we do it internally makes it more difficult to become aware of, yet practicing awareness of what we are telling ourselves is revealing about our belief system and how it pervades our life. We become aware of how we program our limitations, perpetrate our low self-worth and continue to reinforce much of the negative programming we received when we were younger.

What to Say When You Talk to Yourself [7], by Shad Helmstetter, offers many strategies based on affirmations to help break this cycle. Among other concepts, Helmstetter claims that words like "I should, I want, I will try, I can't, I must" are indicative of beliefs that tend to block our learning. In their book *Time Line Therapy* on a strategy derived from neuro-linguistic programming, authors Tad James and Wyatt Woodsmall claim that beliefs are "presuppositions that we have about certain things that either create or deny personal power for us."[8] "I should" and "I must" usually reflect a belief for which we are not taking full responsibility and with which we are not in complete cooperation.

The expression "I want" in Helmstetter's opinion (and I concur) often hides a second subliminal part to the sentence such as "it is impossible" or "they won't let me" that disclaims the intention. "I will try" usually hides a negative projection about the outcome. "I can't" simply refuses participation. Those three expressions—I want, I will try, I can't—betray tentativeness or refusal. As a result, the inner resistance limits full participation in our experiences and this tends to limit what we get out of them. My experience is that replacing these expressions of doubt by " I choose to" raises the commitment level and enriches the learning.

---

[7]   Helmstetter, Shad. What to Say When You Talk to Yourself. Scottsdale, Arizona: Grindler Press, 1986.

[8]   James, Tad and Wyatt Woodsmall. Time Line Therapy and the Basis of Personality. Cupertino, California: Meta Publications, 1988; page 8.

Although these beliefs are potentially limiting, the most restrictive are moral judgments. To classify experiences as right or wrong blocks our ability to derive their substance from them. We no longer look for ways we can use the experience for our advancement, as we are too involved in the process of placing blame and condemnation. It is perfectly appropriate to evaluate our actions as to their effectiveness and learn from the results, but to classify them as good or bad offers little for our upliftment. Very few actions clearly fail in either category. What is obvious from observation is that almost anything can be improved and the worst possible action can be the source of profound learning and transformation. If we could eliminate judgment from our mental arsenal and replace it with acceptance, our ability to learn from life would be profoundly increased.

I am not saying that beliefs are ineffective. Some of our beliefs may indeed lead us in positive directions. What is important to confront is that many of our beliefs are dysfunctional. They lead only to guilt and condemnation and do not help us in our personal development. To be willing to challenge our beliefs or have them challenged by others can be a great source of learning. We no longer need to hold them as absolute. We can enter into an ongoing conversation with ourselves and others in which our beliefs are openly expressed yet are open to change based on solid new evidence. Thus, our beliefs become temporary landmarks in our search for meaning rather than permanent institutions that rule every aspect of our lives.

From a social point of view, communications are healed when we simply look at our beliefs and the beliefs of others as points of view, a way of looking at the situation or the context. A metaphor for this approach is the story of different people looking at a multicolored beach ball. Each person can see some of the colors, but no one sees all the colors. Because our beliefs are often caught in our unconscious, we may be rather blind to reality. The analogy of four blind men describing an elephant might shed some light. One caught the tail and described it as a rope. The other caught the trunk and described it as a hose. The next got the leg and called it a tree trunk, and the fourth got the belly and described it as a huge vat. All are correct in their awareness but limited in their overall experience. Such are most of our beliefs—they are possibly accurate to some degree but highly limited.

Affirmations

As mentioned earlier, one of the effective ways to transform dysfunctional beliefs, when we become aware of them, is to replace them with affirmations. Because most beliefs are implanted in our psyche through repetition and reinforced by self-talk, we can create active sentences that naturally increase our personal power; we can practice repeating them on a regular basis to help us access our inner resourcefulness. The following are some affirmations that I have found particularly helpful in reprogramming limiting beliefs in critical areas of our psyche. An effective way is to repeat these affirmations 100 times daily for 21 days.

Affirmations are useful in working to release hurt and open the heart:

- I am loving myself unconditionally.
- I am standing in the strength of my loving.
- I am openly giving and receiving.

Affirmations to release judgments and open to Spirit:

- I am clearly seeing the beauty in everything and everyone, including myself.
- I forgive all the judgments I hold against myself or anyone else in relationship to anything I have experienced in the past, that I am experiencing in the present, or that I am afraid to experience in the future.

Affirmation to release false pride:

- I am fully acknowledging my inner beauty.

Affirmations to release excessive self-criticism and perfectionism:

- I am fully appreciating myself.
- I am allowing myself to experiment freely.
- I welcome every new challenge as an opportunity to grow and learn.
- I am standing in the strength of my sensitivity, and I am allowing the world to support me.

Affirmations to allow creative expression and playfulness:

- I am allowing the full expression of my creativity.
- I am allowing the full expression of my playfulness.
- I am allowing the full expression of my resourcefulness.
- I am fully expressing the playfulness of Spirit.

Affirmations to increase clarity:

- I am clearly seeing my purpose in life.
- I am clearly seeing my direction in life.

- I am clearly seeing my calling in life.
- I am clearly seeing my mission in life.

Affirmations to break away from other people's expectations:

- I am free to be me.
- I am daring to express my uniqueness.
- What people think of me is not my business.

Affirmation to release indolence:

- I am fully attuning to the Spirit within me.

Of course, you can make affirmations about everything from changing your self-image to making more money, and all affirmations may work to reprogram ineffective beliefs. The reason I have selected the above affirmations is that I have tested them using muscle testing (applied kinesiology) and they are programmed to release tension in specific parts of the body. They strengthen a core structure that acts as a support for many aspects of the psyche.

Attitudes

Attitudes are the byproduct of the impact of our beliefs on our emotions and have a profound impact on our behavior. We saw in the chapter on the Inner Mother that our emotions have the power to mobilize or inhibit our resourcefulness. They are the power behind our involvement or lack thereof. Our attitudes reflect the degree of caring or resistance with which we approach situations and our actions and how we respond to challenges.

Attitudes are a habitual emotional response associated with an underlying belief system, so there is a close connection between the Inner Mother and the Inner Grandparents.

Attitudes are not necessarily bad. Many in fact may have a positive impact on our lives. For example, the attitude of gratitude naturally opens the heart and invariably increases our ability to draw meaning, knowledge and wisdom from our life experiences. Examples of other beautiful attitudes that naturally serve us are respect, attentiveness, consideration for others' needs and open-mindedness. Attitudes that reflect our negative thinking or as some call it our "stinking thinking" typically sound like, "Poor me," "Why me?" "Fuck you," "Who cares?" "So what," "It's not worth it," "This can wait," "Let them do it," "Everybody does it," "Take care of me and fuck you," "What's in it for me anyway." All of these attitudes—gross or subtle, explicit or carefully hidden—reflect our self-worth, our sense of fairness, the hurt we have accumulated in the past, our beliefs in our abilities or our willingness to move out of our comfort zones to embrace or promote change.

Let us look at how emotions and beliefs combine to form some of the above-mentioned attitudes. "Poor me" combines the emotions of hurt and discouragement with the belief that "I can't do anything to change the situation." "Why me?" combines the emotion of resentment with the belief people are deliberately singling me out to pick on. "Fuck you" combines feelings of rage, anger or hate with the belief of "I don't need anybody." "Who cares?" combines the emotions of hurt and resentment with the belief that "No matter what I do, people will still not be happy." "This can wait" or "I'll do it tomorrow" hides the feeling of impotence with the belief that things are not as bad as they seem. As we see, negative attitudes are an attempt at pushing the responsibility for our lives onto someone else or refusing to take charge.

Any one of us who has been around teenagers, either as parents or teachers, are well aware of the impact of attitudes on behavior and learning. Teenagers are well known for their attitude problems, in part because they are defining their own values and are not yet clear about what they want to be involved with, to what degree, and how. Also, it is easier to react to things negatively than to risk experiencing fully what is available to us. Whatever the reason, and there are probably many more that I have not mentioned, negative attitudes tend to limit teens' ability to grow and learn. At their age this is not absolutely critical because it just represents a natural crisis point between childhood, where they depended primarily on their parents to take care of their lives, and adulthood, when they will become responsible for the outcomes of their behavior.

It would be a mistake to assume that negative attitudes are the domain and privilege of the young. We can all benefit from reflecting on our attitudes and their impact on our behavior. Yet, most of us hate to be told that our attitude is getting in our way.

In his book *What to Say When You Talk to Yourself,* Shad Helmstetter emphasizes strongly the importance of beliefs and the unconscious in relation to attitude and behavior. In his opinion, we have to address what is causing the attitude in order to change it and his prescription is to use affirmations.[9] I have

---

[9]   Helmstetter, Shad. What to Say When You Talk to Yourself. Scottsdale, Arizona: Grindler Press, 1986.

also found that, to a large degree, our attitudes respond to our ability to perceive visually.

My experience working with a technique of bodywork called Neural Organization Technique demonstrated to me that unless someone can perceive a positive outcome visually, their level of involvement is going to be minimal and this will be reflected in their achievements or lack thereof. In working with learning dysfunctions, Dr. Carl Ferreri discovered that many children were failing because they could not see themselves succeeding. He discovered a trigger point on the skull that activated a visual reflex. By stimulating that point while suggesting to a child a positive outcome, the child's achievement in school started improving greatly. Not surprisingly, their attitude responded practically instantly, shifting from making constant excuses for themselves to being enthusiastic and motivated.[10]

Our attitude improves dramatically when we have a clear vision of what we want, when the steps we take are proportional with our ability to achieve, and when we experience enough success to motivate ourselves to maintain our effort.

When our attitude starts slipping, we need to examine our feelings and ascertain clearly what they may be communicating. We need to look at our self-talk to find out if we are giving ourselves enough acknowledgment or whether we are always talking to ourselves from a place of discontent and criticism. We need to examine the image we have of the outcome of our actions

---

[10]　Ferreri, Dr. Carl, director and founder of the Neural Organization Technique Institute, 3850 Flatlands Ave., Brooklyn, NY 11234.

and our place in it, and we must look at our level of commitment to what we are doing.

The quality of our learning in life tends to be in direct relationship to our level of involvement. From that to which we give little, we receive little. My spiritual mentor and friend John-Roger, in referring to our level of participation, says that "100 percent is a breeze and anything below that is a bitch." My experience is that often when my attitude toward an action or involvement is not very good, it is because I am afraid to fail. When I am willing to take the risk and challenge my fear, my level of learning is always tremendous, independent of the outcome. If I succeed, I gain great validation and a new outlook on my abilities. If I fall short I gain insight into how far I can go when I give it a hundred percent and a clear picture of the areas that still need improvement.

To take refuge in a negative attitude is a way of refusing to be responsible for our life and finding excuses for our negative outcomes. It is a way of refusing life and the part we came to play in it. By doing this, we deny both the knowledge and wisdom we can gain from our involvement.

Assumptions

In our search for knowledge and meaning, when we were little children, we asked many questions. Some people probably even thought we asked too many questions and got irritated and perhaps they ridiculed us or decided we were not asking the right question. Or, maybe they felt they had answered our question enough times and made it clear by now we should know the answer. Whatever it was, we got a message that to be smart, educated and sophisticated (and to avoid ridicule, failure and pain), we had to pretend we could know what was going to happen before it did. So we started approaching our lives with an increasing number of assumptions. Some of these we made up ourselves based on generalization and linear projection. We took our experience and generalized it so that, if a parent or teacher or one of our friends betrayed us once, we inferred that we could not trust them ever again. If we were hurt once through an experience, we declared it risky and dangerous instead of looking at how we could make it safe, growth-producing and even fun.

How many of us have approached an interview with apprehension, maybe even terror or panic, based on a scenario we created inside ourselves? Then we went there and the situation unfolded in a totally different way than the one we had projected? How many times have we avoided a communication because we assumed we would be rejected or misunderstood or someone would make fun of us? One of my teachers, Dr. Don Klein[11], has done extensive research on the process of humiliation and how profoundly it pervades our lives. If we have been seriously humiliated as a child, we tend to constantly project that fear into our interaction with our external environment.[11]

Assumptions do not work only in terms of projecting negative outcomes. How many times do we expect a certain type of response from somebody—consideration, caring, or special

---

[11] Klein, Don, staff faculty, The Union Institute, P. O. Box 85315, Cincinnati, OH 45201.

attention—only to find them preoccupied or unavailable? This usually results in being disappointed, hurt, angry, resentful or scared, as if our world has collapsed.

Our assumptions seem to be forever running in one direction or another. It is as if we create a world in our creative imaginations, in which we assign roles to ourselves and other people with whom we interact. We create scenarios, dialogues and postures, and we expect life to unfold according to our scenarios. When the scenario is uplifting and flexible enough to allow us to learn from our experiences in a spirit of adventure and revelation, we use the gift of imagination to our advantage. However, many of us use that ability to isolate from new experiences by prejudging the process or the outcome and opting out before we have a chance to fully experience what is available to us.

Assumptions interfere with our ability to live and learn because we rely on information from the past to prejudge a present or future experience. I do not advocate living in an inner world of make-believe and fantasies, but I do encourage you to dare to enter into new experiences (which are not intrinsically destructive) and experience them fully in a spirit of growth and learning.

During my own process of self-exploration, I became aware that I had progressively eroded a beautiful quality from my childhood: my naiveté. I had confused being naive with being dumb or not informed to such a degree that the naiveté of others irritated me. Progressively, I have learned to reclaim my naiveté, to cherish it and experience more situations in my life as an ongoing adventure where I am willing to face the unknown and discover what life makes available to me. In doing this, I am constantly surprised at my abilities and the wealth of resources present at every moment whether the situation is ecstatic, challenging or extremely trying. I find myself asking questions I would have never dared ask for fear of being judged stupid and sharing my own insight without excessive concern for what others may think of me. I approach people with a great deal of love and respect and I honestly share myself, leaving to them the choice of their own response. An affirmation I have used a lot and that helped me a great deal in this process is: "I am fully appreciating my naiveté, and I am approaching new experiences in my life, free of assumptions."

Wisdom

We have seen how wisdom relates to the Grandparents in our Inner Family and how it increases our quality of being. I believe that in this world wisdom has been shortchanged at the expense of knowledge. I like to look at every experience in my life as a teacher, an opportunity to expand, to grow, to enrich myself.

At one time in my life when I was confused about my career, I took a workshop with John C. Crystal a renowned unorthodox career planner and coauthor of *Where Do I Go from Here With My Life?*[12] As part of our homework we were asked to write our autobiography. On one side of the page, we were asked to list all the major experiences we remembered from birth until that point in our life. On the other side of the page, in front of

---

[12] Crystal, John C. The work of John C. Crystal is the inspiration behind the popular book *What Color Is Your Parachute?* by Richard Nelson Bolles, Berkeley, California: Ten Speed Press, 1989.

each experience, we wrote the skills we had learned and how effectively we had mastered them. Crystal explained to us that by the age of 18 everyone who had gone to school had learned all the basic skills needed for any job; we may just not have mastered them to the same degree. That exercise was very revealing to me and improved my self-worth by allowing me to acknowledge myself for the quality of my life learning.

In suggesting this exercise to my clients, I became aware of a missing piece. Another column needed to be added to include the quality or qualities that were revealed through the experiences. I realized, for example, that studying mathematics barely improved my skills, yet it definitely taught me acceptance, persistence and compassion. Similarly, challenging experiences teach us courage, resilience and strength. Taking care of young children tends to reveal sensitivity, empathy, playfulness and spontaneity. I am aware that I have mastered many of my greatest qualities by such seemingly indirect means.

I perceive wisdom as the progressive mastery of the deep qualities of the heart through the process of our life experience. In my opinion, the true purpose of life is to learn how to love and, more specifically, how to love unconditionally. I have found people with a minimum of schooling who were masters at it and many people with power, position and academic degrees who knew very little about love. I have realized that as we become involved in the process of learning to love, we simultaneously start loving to learn, and life becomes a beautiful process of unfolding our uniqueness and sharing it with others. I see that in an era of rapid change, our knowledge fades away rapidly but the wisdom of our heart endures to the end. In our search for meaning, it is important to realize that the most profound learning emerges from within and that life is our true teacher.

Challenging Emotions Associated with the Dynamics of the Inner Grandparents

We are often disturbed by circumstances and behaviors that are unfamiliar or that we do not understand. Similarly, not feeling understood produces a great deal of anxiety. When we lack physical control of our environment, we will often settle for understanding the cause or the mechanism involved in what is happening rather than being satisfied or fulfilled.

A situation that often baffles us is death. Because we have no conscious reference points for what takes place after death, we are often disturbed, feeling left out and abandoned when someone dies. Circumstances and behaviors that defy our understanding promote in us a sense of anxiety, disorientation and loss. Feeling left out, ostracized or simply misunderstood can provoke a high level of anxiety. This anxiety tends to promote unusual behavioral patterns, such as pretending nothing has happened, withdrawing into solitude, compulsively latching onto certain memories or engaging in destructive or self-destructive actions. Sadness, grief and sorrow are the most common emotions at these times.

Grief

Although grief is most common in a period of bereavement due to a death, it can occur as a result of any loss. Any sense of irretrievable loss tends to produce grief. Any major loss threatens the known pattern of our world as we perceive it and which we then attempt to control through understanding.

Grief can be intense. It shatters our abstract reality and forces us to adjust our conceptual framework. It is as if we have to reconstruct a new reality for ourselves and the task can seem so monumental we get stuck in the loss, refusing to accept the new reality presented to us.

Grief is usually compounded by the fact that one loss tends to remind us of others, then we are faced with reliving all of the losses we have previously experienced. When my father died, my mother was not only processing his departure but also reliving the death of my older brother who died at the end of World War II. Recently my spiritual teacher passed, and I went through an intense phase of grieving for my parents and my late wife. In our subconscious mind, all losses seem to be connected and trigger each other.

Each time we lose someone through death, we confront our own mortality. What could more deeply affect our sense of reality? Grief is a reflective process on the nature of reality. What is real or not real? Is nothing permanent? Is everything transient? This profound existential quest touches so deeply all aspects of our world that, whether we are aware or not, we react with the totality of our being.

Grief seems to include a multitude of other emotions: fear, panic, terror, guilt, resentment, rage, anger, hate, worry and many more. We may not be aware of all these emotions, but all of them come up at one moment or another, sometimes expressed yet often denied.

Many factors affect how easily and how long the grieving process takes. One of these is the level of autonomy of those who are left behind. The greater the level of psychological entanglement, the harder is the work of restructuring a reality that does not involve the physical presence of the lost one. Another factor is the quality of the relationship we had with the person who left and the quality of the relationship we have with ourselves and the people who are still here.

Some people flourish after the death of their mate, as if they had been in jail and were suddenly free. More frequently, people have a hard time because they judge the relationship could have been better. Either they blame themselves for not doing all they could while the person was alive or they feel angry that the death robbed them of the opportunity to be with a loved one. My saving grace after the passing of my late wife, Roberta, in 2012 was the immense gratitude I have for the 47 creative years we had together. This gratitude, which is often the final phase of the grieving process, was my starting point. Her loss was, of course, challenging, but I had no doubt about my ability to move forward and create a new life for myself.

Another factor having profound impact is the belief system we have about death. People who believe in some sort of life after death do not seem to react with the same sense of loss as those who see death as the end of it all. In either case, the need is to let go of the past and use our present support system to move forward. It may be as simple as asking for assistance from the people who are still in our life.

I came back from France in August 2012 after putting my late wife's ashes in the family grave in Normandy, desolate after leaving my family in France and feeling lonely in facing the next steps of my life. My approach, which I think had great genius, was to go to a meeting of friends and open up my heart to them. I remember telling them I was available for breakfast, lunch, dinner, movies, theater, concerts and hikes. This simple act opened up deeper relationships with some. One of those who had lost her husband a few years earlier reached out to me. We started doing things together and before long, we realized we were dating. We have now been married for two years and have an amazing relationship. I am not suggesting that this would happen for everyone, but I am clear that if I had not embraced my situation and shared my needs openly, this might never have happened for me.

There are those who experience death as evidence that life is futile, moving into a state of despondency and despair. The process is often similar in cases of separation and divorce, especially but not exclusively on the part of the one who did not desire that outcome.

Most effective in any loss is to focus on what was learned through that relationship. Since true learning is an internal transformation, what we grieve is still inside us in the form of a certain quality, learning or inner strength. The best way to honor the memory of those who have left is to claim for ourselves the gifts they gave us and forgive their limitations and our own.

Although we cannot relive the past, we can learn from it and move on.

In this context, the experience of grieving becomes a celebration of life and a constant opportunity to learn and grow. Each time our outer world is shattered, there is an opportunity to create a new world and explore new possibilities. Death or separation is never an easy process. However difficult it may be, death can be as beautiful as life and a phenomenal growth experience when we choose to approach it with honesty and gratitude.

When we understand that whatever is enduring in a person's legacy is always alive, we can focus on living our lives enriched by their presence rather than claim that what was precious about them was buried with their physical form.

Sadness

Sadness is similar to grief in that it is based on a sense of separation. Grief relates to a permanent loss, but in sadness there is a sense that things could change or could have been different. We often feel sad when relationships, situations or events are not living up to, or have not lived up to, our expectations. In sadness there is also a giving up but not of the same magnitude as grief and not necessarily permanent. If the person or the situation is still present in our life, the feeling of sadness can be even more excruciating because we may irrationally hang onto the possibility that things will change and the connection or good times will be restored. In the long run, the constant disappointment is corrosive and can provoke real despair.

There is also often an unknowing—"How could this be possible? How could they do that to me?"—and a sense we have been left behind. This feeling is common in older people who feel that the times, their children or grandchildren have left them behind. They frequently feel misunderstood, disconnected, unloved and uncared for. We find the same feeling in young children left at school or at camp—feeling disoriented, lost and abandoned. Sadness is a pervasive emotion in our society where foundations of trust and mutual support have been eroded and people are often assessed by their appearance or the size of their wallet rather than on the depth of their feelings, expression and contributions.

As with grief, sadness is a call for action, for moving forward, dedication, self-support and choosing to accept each new situation and every new challenge as an opportunity to grow and learn.

Reflection and introspection—the process of going inward to gain greater knowledge—are essential qualities that allow growth, transformation and gratitude. Self-absorption, the compulsive focus on the negative with no commitment to transformation and self-pity all deny us the richness of life. Sadness is egging us to move on, to create a new vision, to awaken our creative talents and to take responsibility for sharing ourselves and for the quality of our lives. It is a call for action and daring.

Sorrow and Nostalgia

Both of these emotions are anchored in the past. Sorrow is the emotional response to regret, the mental process that looks back at the past with a critical, reactive point of view. It looks at the past through the eyes of the present, denying that the present wisdom is the result of the experiences it is now regretting or condemning. Each experience we have is a piece of our learning. It is an opportunity for growth and transformation. The experience itself is much less important than what we got out of it. Horrendous actions may be the source of great realization. Unfortunately, we have been brought up in a world quick to condemn or praise, which is quite short on reflection. It emphasizes good or bad and constantly grades the result at the expense of what is being learned.

Occasionally, immediate results may clearly reflect lessons to be learned. Usually, the truly profound learning is hidden and the depth of the experience may not be related to the situation or subject matter. I learned to stand up for myself through stating my love of Johann Sebastian Bach in an English class in which the teacher, for whom I had great admiration, did not like Bach. I have learned a great deal of humility, discipline, precision and surrender in handling financial matters and little about investment. I have learned courage in studying mathematics and little about math.

Life is a constant source of learning, and our greatest learning often comes disguised in the form of our greatest challenges or our most memorable failures. Rather than look back with sorrow, we need to bring our wisdom to bear in the present to heal the wounds inflicted through our past. We can exercise gratitude for the countless opportunities to learn. If we use our stumbling blocks as stepping stones, life can be greatly enriched and we can move on to new lessons and discovery. If we deny the richness of the lessons and the opportunities to learn, we are probably busy setting up a similar lesson to be learned in a new guise.

Sorrow is located in the body in the lower belly, the area the mystics called the "hara," "dantian" or "ki" center—the power center. Whenever we deny learning from the past and interpret it as good or bad, it undermines our personal power and foundation.

While sorrow is based in regret, nostalgia is also an attachment to the past and a denial of the present. In this case, the regret is that whatever it was, it has ended. Nostalgia says, "If only it could be as beautiful as when . . .," "I wish I were still . . .," "In my time . . . .," etc.

Here again, learning is being denied. Our left-brain hemisphere, which is sequential and chronological, plays a nasty trick on us. Because it organizes our experiences in sequence, we have a tendency to believe that what we gained or learned from an experience disappears with the experience. Yet we all learned our multiplication tables when we were in third or fourth grade and we still remember them. Why not look at the rest of our experiences the same way?

Claiming the Blessings Exercise

Here is a simple exercise to illustrate the point.

Close your eyes and focus on a time in your life
that was precious to you. Let go of any sense that
it is gone and allow yourself to totally immerse
yourself in it. How does it feel? What is the quality
or qualities you truly appreciate about it? Where
do you experience this quality right now? It is
inside you, of course! Everything you experience
is inside you. The situation that so appealed to you
only catalyzed or amplified a state of being that
was always present inside of you. If that state is so
precious to you, recall the past situation and bring
it forward inside yourself now. Now commit to
bringing that quality into your life in a greater way.

Let me give you a personal experience that also illustrates this
point. A number of years ago, I left the French Embassy, where
I had been working for seven and a half years, to practice my
new calling as a body-mind therapist. I proceeded to fall in
love with the new California environment. After my training,
I moved back to the East Coast of the United States, hoping
I would quickly make my way back to California. Because of
financial limitations and the need to provide a steady learning
environment for my children, we stayed for approximately

fourteen years in Connecticut. I spent several years wishing I were out West. The result of this persistent nostalgic feeling was that I was not truly involved in my work and was not very successful. That, of course, made me wish even more that I lived in California.

Finally, I wised up and asked myself what California represented for me. It represented adventure, peace and flowing with my own rhythm. I reflected on how I could bring forward more of these qualities in my life in Connecticut. It was definitely more difficult to do this on my own than to respond to the environment. I created some affirmations, made some changes in my life and created a nice support system for myself by going to meet the people in my area who were working along the same lines of interest. As a result, my work improved and the financial stress decreased. When the time came that I could move back West, I decided that, at least for the time being, I liked where I was and there were many things I wanted to complete before I would be ready to move.

By being willing to claim that the qualities I was missing were inside me rather than outside, I was able to change my life and bring it more into alignment with my vision.

All of the emotions that relate to the movement of knowing, the Inner Grandparents, have to do with what we need to learn and how we cooperate with the learning. Because of our cultural emphasis on cognitive learning as the highest form of learning, we often forget that the whole process of life is about learning. Indeed, learning is the essence of happiness, transformation and personal growth.

Every situation in our lives, large or small, is there for a purpose— to assist us in fulfilling our potential and realizing the totality of who we are. The word "education" is derived from the Latin "educare," which means to draw forth from within. This clearly indicates that the bulk of learning is a process of recognition— realizing that we already possess all essential knowledge. Our life experiences are here to help us claim that knowledge. When children are not properly acknowledged or feel misunderstood, they will strive for recognition. Since cognitive knowledge is valued so highly in our society, many children may pursue academic achievement. However, most of academia denies that the source of knowledge is within, so that child often is led into a dead end. Feelings of separation continue and personal relationships suffer.

To claim that knowledge is already within and is revealed through our life experiences opens up a new dimension to living. Every type of learning is viewed with respect and gratitude. We can do away with intellectual arrogance! I will always remember the ecstasy experienced by my first son when, in eleventh grade, he discovered how simple it was to write about and share his own experience. I remember his equal dismay in following years when his teachers insisted on an academic format that rewarded mental gymnastics over his own innate inner knowledge. Since then, as a student at Stanford University, I am sure he has mastered the game of impressing other scholars. I just hope in my heart he has not forgotten the impact of his experience and how beautiful it is to simply share the richness of his own life experience. Many of the people who have touched me the most deeply in my life, were people who had little formal education but who knew the value of their own life experience.

To Live Fully

—

What good are these hands
if I do not run them through the hair
of my beloved children?

What good are these eyes
if I do not drink in the landscape
for the sheer pleasure of drunkenness?

What good are these ears
if I do not listen for the rhythmic tread
of elephants and ants?

What good are these legs
if I do not run barefoot
through the cool morning grass?

What good is this tongue
if I do not taste the salty brine
of the boundless ocean in which I swim?

What good is this voice
if I do not proclaim through song and sound
all that I know to be true?

What good is this body
if I do not dance unfettered
all the stories of my passing days?

And what good is this heart,
Dear One,
if I do not love
as if tomorrow will never come?

Chapter Seven

THE DYNAMICS
OF THE INNER CHILD
Loving to Live

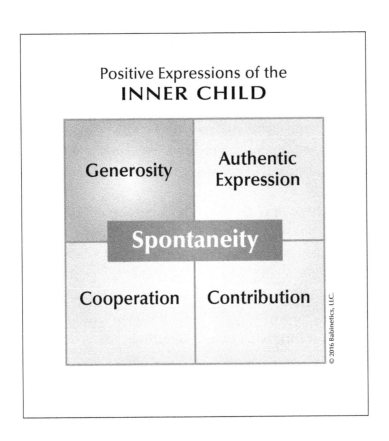

In looking at the Inner Family in the Chinese tradition, the Child is related to the wood element; the season is Spring, and it is associated with the wind; the main organs are the liver and gallbladder, which are said to open into the eyes. The wood function and its corresponding organs are often compared to a general in the army. This role of the general is to defend the national territory and to go out to conquer more land for expansion. Like the wind, the Child inside of us is spontaneous, sometime erratic and even reckless. To be healthy, the energy of the Child needs to be supported by the clarity and reliability of the Father, the compassion of the Mother and the wisdom of the Grandparents. Yet despite any shortcomings, the Child is the true spirit of life. In most cultures we worship the beauty of youth because young people carry the seeds of the future. Often, however, the challenge that youth and creativity represent to our traditions and comfort frightens us. We sometimes try to resist or destroy the seeds of renewal within ourselves and in others.

The greatest asset of the Child is its creative imagination. The Child has the ability to dream new worlds, overcome all obstacles and conquer new territory. Yet many children, when they grow older, lose the ability to create. Like many adults, they become overly cautious and reasonable, unwilling to take chances and more concerned with the defense of known territory than the extension of their boundaries and learning.

When I meet or visit older people, I am struck by the few who still seem to carry a marveling child inside of them. In spite of their age they look as if they were just born and their spirits are full of joy and life. They welcome new things with excitement, maintain a beautiful relationship with younger people and are always ready for a laugh. Their youthfulness is an inspiration.

What differentiates these people from the ones who grow "old" is the power of their imagination. No matter how restricted their bodies may be (and I have seen some who could hardly talk anymore, let alone walk), their eyes tell the story. They are fully alive in their inner vision. They are singing with the singers, dancing with the dancers, running with the runners and reveling in all the mischief of the young. My kind of people! God, how I love them! When looking at them, I always reflect on how they keep their creative imagination so alive.

The first thing I discovered talking to these people is that none of them were chasing fantasies. All of them had had a life full to the brim with experiences, and they were bringing their lives to a completion with no regrets. They were proud of their accomplishments and, even in the present moment, were looking toward tomorrow with excitement.

Imbalances in our ability to create our world the way we want are the result of a block that affects one of the four basic dynamics of the Inner Family: preservation, authenticity, learning and contribution. Confusion between fantasy and reality affects our drive for creative self-expression.

Fantasy vs. Reality

The creative imagination is a beautiful gift. It is most effectively used when connected to reality. For example, running a four-minute mile was considered humanly impossible for many decades. The fact that it is commonplace among top runners nowadays is a tribute to the creative genius of the first one who did it, Roger Bannister. In that act he opened up the imaginations of those who followed him, but this accomplishment is still reserved for runners who are naturally talented and who have trained extensively toward that goal and beyond. For most of us, it is not a realistic goal because we do not have the drive and/or the physical ability to fulfill it.

People who confuse fantasy and reality usually place their expectations unreasonably high for their ability level and/or they want immediate results. I often show my clients a tree in the far distance. I ask them how long it takes them to imagine themselves at the foot of the tree. Most tell me "instantly." I then ask them how long it would take them to run to the tree. Of course, it is substantially longer. Then I ask them how much effort it took to imagine being there and they say "not much." Then I ask them to reflect on their physical conditioning and ask them how hard it would be for them to run there. Although the last answer may vary greatly depending on their physical condition, they all agree that imagining an action is easier and faster than actually doing it.

This points out two important keys in learning how to more effectively use our creative imaginations. One is that it works better to set realistic expectations. Second is to be prepared to walk (or run!) the road. My experience in life is if you want something, you have to be willing to take the actions that lead you there. Unwillingness or inability to act leaves us in the field of fantasy.

I have seen many people stuck in the pattern of confusing fantasy with reality. There is often great beauty around them when they are younger and full of lofty ideals. However, they often fail to walk the road that leads to success because they feel it is too hard. Either they lack self-confidence or they believe the world owes it to them and should deliver what they want on a silver platter. Their constant failure at reaching their visions and goals, along with a lack of appreciation for the beauty of the process, tends to make them dissatisfied, frustrated and bitter. As they get older, they become more and more reluctant to take the steps they need to take to reach the outcomes they see for themselves. Instead, they involve their creative talents in making up elaborate excuses for themselves and use their enthusiasm to convince others how much they have tried to no avail or how unlucky they have been. They end up in the role of victims of life circumstances.

It is essential for each one of us to create a lofty vision for ourselves that inspires us and is likely to generate a sense of fulfillment. As we walk along our path in life, we can support ourselves more effectively by breaking down our vision into smaller steps (goals or major milestones) that we can easily visualize in their completion. By staying in touch with what is genuinely reachable for us, we increase our experience of success, maintain our involvement and support our ongoing commitment. One key in doing this is to avoid vagueness in setting our goals. The more specific we are in our vision, the easier it is to visualize the process. Ambiguity breeds confusion and uncertainty generates anxiety while promoting procrastination.

Self-Image

In the Inner Family, the creative imagination is ruled by the Child, and it is profoundly influenced by our childhood experiences. Those who experienced a great deal of success when they were young and receive acknowledgment for their skills usually approach new tasks with excitement and a great deal of confidence in their abilities. Those of us who experienced falling short of our goals and/or endured much unloving criticism tend to approach new tasks with apprehension.

We construct images from millions of small impressions gathered from our life experience as children and our genetic conditioning. This process starts early in the womb and is particularly active during our earlier years when we are very impressionable. It involves a representation of ourselves, other people, and the place we occupy in the world. This tends to delineate for us a sphere of comfort or at least of familiarity that acts as a reference point for what we can or cannot do. Although that representational system can be modified throughout our lives, it plays a profound role in our perception of reality.

Any challenge to that familiar reference point tends to produce high levels of anxiety. Rather than face the discomfort, we often resort to mental strategies to reaffirm the impossibility of breaking through our self-imposed limitations. Shifting our self-image can be particularly challenging. When our childhood was traumatic, insecurity expands exponentially. Individuals who experienced major trauma have a great deal more trouble dealing with anxiety and ambiguity. As a result, they are less prone to challenging and expanding their comfort zone.

It is easy to recognize pathological manifestations of this imbalance in people who have a weak or highly distorted sense of self, but it is harder to appreciate how the image we create of our reality has a profound impact on our own behavior. Even though the handicap may have been overcome or our natural resilience and fortuitous gifts may have partially cancelled the negative feedback we received, we may still to some extent project reality the way we experienced it when we were children. Our self-talk may also reflect that old reality. Therefore, it is important to educate our Inner Child to the fact that things have changed and the resources at our disposal now are very different from those we had when we were younger.

We have the option to consistently support ourselves in our efforts and reward ourselves for our achievements. Through positive visualization, affirmation and taking steps to challenge our limitations, we can progressively alter our self-image while building strong success strategies. Success tends to breed confidence and alter the images we hold of ourselves as well as the place we can occupy in the world.

I remember a walk I took as a child on my parents' farm in Normandy, France. I was approximately seven years old and the field was absolutely huge and full of thistles. The walk seemed endless, and I was exhausted when I got home. Since then I have done that same walk probably a hundred times, usually in less than ten minutes. The walk is the same, yet my relationship to it is vastly different. Due to numerous repetitions, an old reference point has been replaced with a new one. I do not approach that walk with apprehension. Each time I walk it, I am still surprised at how short it truly is.

Similarly, many people at age 30 or 40 still perceive themselves as the fat kid they were when they were 12 years old. They may be beautifully elegant and slender now. Yet a part of them still feels fat because they did not correctly communicate to the Child within that it had done a good job in achieving their ideal weight.

A big key in improving our self-image is to add acknowledgment to success. For fear of being judged as bragging, many of us have learned to underplay our achievements and not reward ourselves for what we have completed. We often expect other people to do this for us but we seldom, if ever, do it for ourselves. This simple lack of gratitude to ourselves for our abilities, gifts, talents or simply our courage and hard work, is like a physical blow we administer to ourselves. It does not produce humility, as we may have been taught, but simply hurts the Child within and inhibits our natural desire to do good work.

Biofeedback has shown that with simple feedback in the form of a beep or a light, we can almost effortlessly learn how to regulate our heartbeat or our brain waves. In the same way, feedback through acknowledgment and simple appreciation reinforce our self-image and increases our sense of empowerment.

It is so important for each member of the Inner Family to truly communicate with each other. As children we were often ordered around and talked at rather than conversed with. As a result we tend to push our Child around and provide it with a minimal amount of positive feedback, expecting it to grasp every new nuance without clear communication.

The concept of self-image is often used interchangeably with self-worth, self-esteem or self-concept. They are intimately interlinked, but in fact reflect different modes we use to access reality. Self-image reflects the impressions obtained through the visual mode. Self-esteem and self-worth reflect how we feel about ourselves. Self-concept represents how we articulate our perception into words. Those specific aspects of self perception are directly related through the visual, kinesthetic and auditory modalities through which we connect with our environment.

In restoring or expanding our positive self-image, it is important to remember these three modes of perception because what we felt, what we heard and what we saw played a great part in that constructed image of our self. One method particularly effective in reprogramming self-perception is "modeling" or imitating other people's actions, personas or behaviors. A great deal of modeling takes place spontaneously in our lives. When we are children, we tend to model our parents or older siblings. When we are teenagers, we tend to model heroes, movie stars, rock stars, great athletes or the coolest kid in the class.

The choice of whom we model may afterward create positive or disastrous results. When we are older, we may still model ourselves on aspects we perceive in others. The technique of modeling consists of choosing a role model and aligning yourself with the way they look, dress, stand, speak and move. The more you can get into the character, the more effective this becomes. It is important not to see the modeling as yourself acting out someone else, but rather as you exploring another aspect of yourself.

You will discover that the way you look has a profound impact on the way you feel and the kind of inner dialogue you pursue inside. Shifting role models periodically is a good way to explore new facets of your own being. The more people you can model in this way, the greater the flexibility of your own self-expression will be. Just make sure you choose people who are successful and uplifting so you expand beyond your present boundaries.

Another avenue to positive learning, growth and expansion is having a mentor or a coach. A mentor is someone we trust and we look up to, who exemplifies the type of success we would like to achieve in our life. A coach is someone who has been trained to help you achieve your goal by assessing and challenging your limitation and creating success strategies. Short of having found a specific mentor or coach with whom we can create a specific relationship, we can use the modeling process as a way to explore new facets of our beingness, mobilize and practice new qualities and begin expanding our abilities.

Some potentially useful affirmations that support a positive image of yourself might be:

- I am fully radiating my natural grace and beauty.
- I am fully enjoying my graceful and healthy body.
- I am a beautiful woman (handsome man) and I am standing tall within myself.
- I am trusting my inner resources and naturally expressing my talents in every aspect of my life.

Another particularly important key is completion. Whenever I begin to feel less than good about myself, I look at what I have not been doing that I had told myself I would do. I then create a step-by-step plan to complete it. Or I communicate to my Inner Child that we are not going to do that right now and make a new agreement.

For example, it is better for self-worth to "eat like a pig" than tell yourself you are going to diet and not do it. If, however, your weight is a strong self-image issue, join an organization that gives you the support you do not yet know how to give yourself and learn and follow their proven routine. This is far better than emotionally beating yourself up each day. You can extend this to any addictive pattern: compulsive shopping, gambling, drinking, drug use and so forth.

Rewarding yourself is the other fundamental technique in maintaining self-worth. The more we prize and reward ourselves for small accomplishments, the better we feel and the more motivated we are to challenge limitations and explore new avenues of growth. Be sure that your reward is not counterproductive, however, such as eating sweets if you are committed to losing weight. Use something that pleases you but you are not compulsive about like a bubble bath, leisurely walk or back rub from a friend.

Whenever individuals use self-abusive or punitive language, they invariably become afraid of failing and start procrastinating. Such self-talk consistently produces the reverse of what is genuinely intended. Self-acceptance, self-love and consistent reaffirmation generate positive transformation. Self-abuse and punishment in any form may give us some sense of moral rectitude, but in the final analysis, they produce fear, lowered self-worth and negative results. That being said we may have to learn how to overcome built in limitation. Some of those are imagining things to do as more difficult as they really are or projecting negative outcomes

Overcoming Imagining What We Want to Do as Difficult

Some of the challenges in my childhood illustrate how we can be programmed into believing that doing anything new is difficult, if not impossible. I was born during World War II in France, broke my arm at nine months old getting out of my crib, was burned from the back of my knees to my waist when I was 18 months old, and was in the trenches during the bombardment that preceded the disembarkation in Normandy. I had serious problems as a child with fine motor control and dyslexia. I was constantly criticized for my clumsiness and told what an airhead I was. My average grade on most of my school papers was an F due to poor spelling.

Occasional positive comments in the margin about my creativity did little to overcome the feeling of failure. I was faced with challenges that seemed out of proportion to my ability level: the war and its impact, the death of my older brother, my tendency to urinate in bed late into my childhood, as well as my difficulty with learning and coordination. Because I did not know what to do about things that disturbed me, I tried using my intellect to figure out why things happened the way they did. This did not help me handle my life any more easily, and by analysis, I came to believe that things were hard to do and I was not very good at them. With the increased frequency of failures and negative feedback, my willingness to try and give it my best shot decreased. I got more and more stuck in attempting to maintain some level of self-worth by taking refuge in fantasizing and pretending that if I had really tried, it would be different. Eventually I stopped daring to dream or project any vision because I believed that what happened to me was fate and there was not much I could do about it.

I still approach writing with a certain amount of apprehension. As I challenge myself and become progressively better at it, I find myself procrastinating less and approaching it with more excitement than apprehension. I have also been afraid to undertake things like carpentry and house repair because of the frequent remarks from my father about what a klutz I was. The funny thing is that I am rather good at these things and invariably reflect afterward on how much simpler it was than I had anticipated. My late wife, who was well aware of my resistance, found a trick. She would start the project herself then ask for help. Once she got me involved, we either completed the project together or she would pull out and I would finish it by myself. In either case the feeling of satisfaction when it was completed was great.

This is the type of scenario that can be responsible for people imagining things as more complicated than they really are. Although some of my circumstances may have been challenging, I came from a large family and I was surrounded with a great deal of loving and unconditional support for me as a person. I often doubt my abilities, but overall I have pretty solid self-worth.

A complementary factor in my pattern of self-doubt is that I was not coordinated and was surrounded by members of my family who were extremely skillful. They had trouble relating to what I was going through and would frequently take over whatever I was doing. After a while, I understood that if I wanted something done well, it was easier for me to not try real hard and let other people do it for me. That may have gotten me some of the things I wanted, but it did not greatly improve my skills.

Eventually I moved out of those self-limiting patterns by choosing to take risks. I put myself in various social contexts and gave myself a chance to discover new things about myself. I went to live in England for a year and discovered that when I was not surrounded by the expectations of my family, I was quite different. I tried skills I would never have dared at home and often received praise for them. I did construction work, gaining more trust in my strength and abilities. I began studying German and Spanish and went to spend some time in Germany. My gift with languages helped me break through my belief I was not good at studying. When I came to the United States as a student, I went to work in a French restaurant as a waiter. Although I never became a fantastic waiter, I greatly improved my fine motor control. I also started doing yoga, learning to relax and trust my body.

Since then, my life has been one experience after another of challenging my limitations and discovering my strengths, abilities and talents. The willingness to take risks, beginning wherever I am, irrespective of my age or assumptions about what I might be capable of at my stage in life, has helped me overcome difficulties and dramatically changed the way I approach life. I may still imagine things as more difficult than they actually are, but instead of approaching new situations with defeatism, I pursue new learning with the confidence that, given the right amount of time and effort, I will master the skills and knowledge I need to complete what I undertake.

Another approach in handling tasks or challenges that appear difficult is to follow the precept of the great philosopher Descartes. He found that in order to investigate certain phenomena, it was easier to break them down into parts—one of the great abilities of the cognitive mind. This strategy also works well in regard to the creative visual process. When a task appears too complicated, break it down into action steps that are commensurate with your perceived ability level. Do not try to figure out all of the steps at once but concentrate on the next one and use your creative imagination to see yourself completing it the way you want to. When you are finished with that step, focus on the next one and so on. By focusing on one step at a time, you will be amazed at how much you can accomplish. If, in addition, you reward yourself after each accomplishment, your ability to fulfill your dreams without creating great stress will increase dramatically.

Canceling Projecting Negative Outcomes

Few of us consciously set ourselves up to fail or choose negativity as a direction for our lives, but we often do just that on a subliminal level. Characteristics like low self-worth, mentalizing, fantasizing and much of our negative self-talk reflect to us that we are afraid to fail. Fear of failure involves a negative projection. Shockingly, more than 90 percent of our fears are irrational and unfounded. The striving for attention that animates many of our actors and artists often hides a fear of not being enough. The need for recognition that motivates many of our scholars reflects fears of being misunderstood. The pursuit of approval so common among people who act in support of others may indicate a fear of not being lovable, and the pursuit of power and money often belies a deep fear of lack.

The shaky foundation of our unconscious is reflected in numerous conscious and unconscious fears, undermining an ability to hold a strong positive focus. How many good intentions have been cancelled because they were destroyed by doubt? We doubt ourselves, others, the world, God. Doubts are the seeds of our demise; they undermine the vision of our greatness. Because much of this counterproductive activity is happening below the surface of consciousness, we have to be alert and pull the weeds of negativity just as they start growing while simultaneously planting and fertilizing a beautiful new garden of joy, upliftment and success.

Each time you catch yourself thinking or talking about something that is the opposite of what you want to happen, choose to redirect the energy and consciously visualize the outcome you prefer. As you deliberately place your focus on positive outcomes, the weeds of negativity will wither and die and become the fertilizer for beautiful new growth.

Spend some time creating an ideal vision for each of your major projects. You do this by taking one project at a time, visualizing each aspect as you want it to take place, including the outcome, and taking time every day to review each one of these pictures as if it were already complete. You can also reinforce this process by creating a "treasure map." Look around in magazines for pictures or draw or paint pictures that symbolize all the things you would like to see happening in your life. After you have gathered them, assemble them on a wall or on a large board in a way that is meaningful and looks beautiful to you. Give the map a prominent place in your home and spend some time every day looking at it, visiting it, taking a trip in it—as if all the facets it represents were already an active part of your life. Feel free to modify it for the better and to let it grow with you so it always represents accurately your vision of your ideal life.

Most fears are unfounded and the more negative attention we give them, the bigger they grow. Pursue your life with care and consideration for your wellbeing without letting your fears run you. Send a lot of love to the part of you that is afraid and continue walking the path that leads you to the fulfillment of your vision and goals.

There is a saying in Esoteric Science circles that "energy follows thought and form follows focus." This means that what you focus on is what you get. If you find yourself spending much of your time focusing on negative outcomes; unrealistic expectations; imagined undue difficulties; self-perceptions of being weak, sick, incompetent or unlucky; past mistakes and thoughts of war against all the evil, real or imagined, in the world, your focus is on negativity. You might want to consider different choices and focus for your life!

Negativity produces results in your consciousness such as low self-image and poor health. Negative attitudes and ineffective behaviors tend to promote exactly what you want to avoid. If that is the case—to any degree—you have your work cut out for you.

Changing Your Focus Exercise

The following exercise will help change your focus.

1. Focus on what you want to see in your life or in the world.
2. Create a beautiful image of the outcome you want to achieve.
3. Get a sense of how you would feel if your dream had come true.
4. Put the scene into words in the most visual and sensory language you can find while still keeping it short.
5. Create an affirmation that describes you in that scene with the feelings you would have.
6. Substitute the new focus for the old one and continue to reprogram your negative projection until your ideal visions start manifesting in your life.

If you have many negative images, you may have to confront each one of them, creating for each one of them an ideal vision in the manner described above.

An effective affirmation will elicit the vision from which it came. That vision, in turn, will elicit positive self-talk and positive attitudes. This positive energy will tend to manifest in the form of increased motivation and more effective, self-confident behavior. This tends to result in getting more of what you want from your life.

Let me share a dramatic example with you. In 1967 I was hired in the Industrial Analysis section of the French Embassy. My boss was friendly but uncommunicative and tended to isolate himself. The secretaries were very nice; however, I did not command a great deal of respect from them due to my original ways of spelling, and they frequently made fun of me behind my back. Another coworker was a middle-aged man who was waiting for a new job elsewhere. He had absolutely no interest in what he was doing and no desire to assist me in any way.

In a typically French managerial style of the time, I was offered almost no direction, guidance or training. I was supposed to extract from the technical press, in areas about which I knew nothing, the most exciting, current and relevant innovations. I was expected to answer inquiries from French companies on subjects totally foreign to me. To say that I was confused would have been an understatement. I was lost and did not feel very good about myself. In addition, I was a brand-new father, an added responsibility for which no one is ever quite prepared.

After six months a colleague informed me that my boss was not satisfied with my performance and when my trial period was completed they might ask me to leave. I had received absolutely no feedback, no direction, and no acknowledgment or positive reinforcement. At that point I was truly lost and scared.

In desperation I turned to yoga and started attending classes regularly. The class consisted of 30 minutes of exercise, a 15-minute talk on various aspects of life and a short meditation. The second talk I heard was about positive focusing. I remember it because it had such a positive impact on my life. It was suggested that for the following week we become aware of any time we approached anything with a negative attitude. It was recommended that, at that very moment, we consciously redirect our focus to what we truly wanted to have happen in that specific situation. I felt I had nothing to lose, so with all of the commitment that can emerge from what felt like desperation, I started using this technique continually—or at least as often as I was conscious of my negative thoughts.

In the beginning it was challenging because the process seemed endless. I definitely did not feel good about my current life circumstances. In spite of that, each time I caught myself getting negative, I identified what I wanted to happen and focused on that outcome.

The results were amazing. I started understanding what I was actually doing rather than pretending to be a victim of circumstance. I became interested in certain new developments in management, personnel development, marketing, the environment, urban development, urban transit, educational technology and more.

I created a human resource network of experts in industries, research centers, think tanks, consulting firms, governmental agencies and universities that I could access whenever I needed information. Being connected with an invisible think tank increased my effectiveness tremendously. Slowly, I became the person to contact when anyone at the embassy wanted to have information quickly on any trend I was following closely. I published many articles in France and my relationship with my boss became fantastic. In many ways he became my mentor, supporting me in many of my new endeavors.

This may sound like a fairy tale, but I have seen the same story (with different details) reproduced hundreds of times. When people start taking charge of their lives, claiming the fact that they are the writer, director, producer and lead actor in the scenario of their lives, and when they start focusing on what they want rather than projecting negative outcomes and making excuses for their lack of achievement, they become creative human beings with the vision, willingness and courage to fulfill their dreams. When we enrich the process by clarifying our own values and using creative visualization and affirmations, miracles take place, and what seemed impossible just yesterday starts manifesting naturally in our lives.When we allow ourselves to be truly creative in every aspect of our lives, life becomes an incredible adventure. Even when things do not go the way we had planned, it only provides us with more opportunity to be creative. Loving to live is daring to be all that we can be, keeping the Child within alive and allowing our dreams to come true through a clear focus on where we are going and a willingness to walk the path.

Challenging Emotions Associated with the Dynamics of the Inner Child

The Inner Child supports the movement toward freedom through creativity, daring and the belief that anything is possible. When events or people challenge expectations, the Inner Child can rebel, expressing anger, rage, frustration or hate. If the outward manifestation of these feelings is inhibited through fear, they become internalized.

There is a great deal more freedom in our creative imagination than in the physical world. In our dreams we can fly, jump over buildings and much more. The right side of the cortex in our brain rules this creative ability and it thrives on intuition, metaphors and visualization. Through our ability to imagine, we reach beyond the limits of our own experience to explore new areas. We are inspired to discover the strategies and processes that turn fantasies into reality. All major discoveries started with an inspired vision of the possible that defied the common wisdom and reached beyond what appeared probable. The probable is based upon history. The possible starts with a leap of faith into uncharted territory.

Through our innate creative genius—which is an extension of God's creativity—we can escape the limits and boundaries of our present situations. Yet, if we visualize only what we want and do not bring our creativity into a physical form, we can feel even more frustrated than if we had no dreams. Many of us give up our dreams early in life and bury our rage so we can fit within the limited vision presented to us through our environment. Many traditional systems of psychotherapy pursue this very end in order to reduce the clients' aspirations and dreams and allow them to fit neatly into their environment. Thus the expression "shrink" is used to describe the occupation of psychotherapy.

Unfortunately, becoming a "well-adjusted" member of society does not mean that we now have the skills and talents to fulfill our dreams. This difficulty is the major source of the negative emotions pertaining to this movement of our consciousness. Because fulfillment seems so easy in our imagination, we can become impatient with the process of learning and rebel against it. The Child inside likes instant gratification and does not want to learn to practice the discipline that allows freedom.

If you have tried your hand at various creative activities, you may understand when watching somebody who has mastered a skill, that what appears as simple actually has been achieved through work and discipline. Because this movement of the Inner Child is associated with the need for attention, we often settle for the attention and betray our own talent. Daring to express our uniqueness is realizing that we were all invested with Divine gifts. It is our responsibility to master them so we can share them with the world as acts of service and love. When we refuse the process of learning and the discipline and focus that it implies, we avoid the lessons that are continually being presented to us for our upliftment. The emotions of anger, rage, frustration and hate are consequences of the denial of our possibilities.

Anger

Because anger has been so often repressed in our society, most of us are quite uncomfortable when it emerges, and it can be lethal or destructive when unchecked. We, therefore, tend to be afraid of anger. During childhood, our anger may have been ridiculed, admonished or met with physical force or violence in the form of a power struggle that we seldom, if ever, won. We may have attempted to exercise control over our environment through our expression of anger. If those around us did not feel strong enough to match our level of discontent, they either gave in or tried to placate us.

What emerges in these situations is a power struggle involving anger and fear. We either use our anger to try and control our environment when things are not going our way, or we subjugate ourselves to other people who exercise more power. We repress our expression and internalize our anger. Initially, the open expression of anger may appear effective, but in the final analysis, it is usually counterproductive. It promotes a world ruled by force and power as opposed to sharing, exchange, mutual respect, negotiation and cooperation. Eventually the repressed rebels topple their aggressors and start abusing their newfound power. Most conflict in our society is a dance of variations on the theme of fear and anger.

To break free of this fatal pursuit, we need to understand more clearly what anger is about, what it is telling us, and how we can use it for our advancement in a way that does not inflict upon others. Anger is related to the liver and the gall bladder. In Chinese medicine the liver rules the muscles, so we will tend to find the anger locked into specific muscle groups, such as the jaw or fist, arms and shoulder, or the feet and the legs. In other words, the parts of our bodies involved in biting, punching and kicking, as we saw at the beginning of this chapter on the dynamics of the Child. The positive expression of the child is associated with creative expression, spontaneity and fun. It is the energy of spring, of new growth breaking through, of rebirth, but because of this need to be at the center, the child need attention.

The Child movement is toward learning about its creative power and wanting to establish its unique place in our midst. This impetus shows up in children's clamoring to "Pay attention to me; I am important." At times, the insistence on our attention when we are otherwise engaged is irritating, and we can respond with frustration or anger. Children then feel denied and will either subjugate, repress themselves or attempt to match our energy level (of frustration and anger) to get their way. The conflict here is in our priorities. While teaching children they are important beings, it may not be practical or in their best interests to always give them our undivided attention. Still, we need to communicate that their needs, interests, discoveries, and very presence is of great importance to us.

While the need to be the center of attention varies greatly from one child (or adult!) to another, we all want to be heard. Each of us came onto this planet to express our uniqueness, and we all deserve a great deal of attention. The movement of consciousness related to anger is connected with the Inner Child. If the spirit has not been squelched, it is exuberant, expressive and fearless. In too many of us, the creativity and willingness to take risks has been stunted through ridicule or control. As a result, a great deal of anger and apathy are present.

When fresh thinking, new endeavors and personal expansion are needed, anger is often a first step in the right direction. It tells us that we have allowed ourselves to be subjugated by our own fears, by others or by the culture we live in. It calls forward courage to face our limitations and our fears, to dare to be free and to express the totality of who we are.

That will to be free, so present in children and so beautifully expressed in their spontaneity, is what is really hidden behind our anger, frustration, rage and hate. We do not need to be afraid of this beautiful energy. We have to realize that it is potentially explosive and needs to be channeled into uplifting visions. It needs to move beyond the reactive state to a clear affirmation of who we are and the vision we are committed to. Because it is an expression of a need for freedom, it has to be "freedom to" and not "freedom from." "Freedom to" starts with a clear vision that expresses itself in support of others and ourselves, then it is mobilized with the proper strategy and fulfills itself in discipline and follow-through. Rather than clipping our children's wings, we have to trust their vision and help them move beyond their selfishness and resistance to fulfill their destiny. And when we experience our own anger, we have to be willing to reflect on how we are allowing ourselves to be subjugated. We must define our own vision and be willing to support it to completion.

This is not so much a question of "fighting for things" as it is a process of living in our own integrity and affirming what is true for us. Many times, fighting for something is a way of genuinely avoiding going for it. Anger is simply reflecting what internal or external controls are preventing us from fully daring to be who we are. We have to go beyond the need for attention to a true commitment—to a vision and willingness to live and be that vision.

As long as we are not choosing back to our vision or are even too afraid to formulate one of our own, our anger will remind us that we are living in slavery or scarcity. Within us, there is a force that is revolting against that subjugation and screaming to have the courage to be free.

As we have seen above, anger locates itself in the arms, the shoulders, the jaw and the legs. The natural physical instinct that we can see in any child who gets mad is to bite, punch or kick. Anger is puffing the body up, usually in the chest, to make us look bigger and deter an opponent invading our territory and threatening our freedom. But it also contracts, tightens and clenches preparing us to fight the enemy. We have to learn to channel that energy by creating the proper strategies to fully establish and express our uniqueness.

There are three other emotions related to anger: rage, frustration and hate. They are all concerned with our desire to express and be received and are based on our vision of what place we want to occupy in the world. This vision may not be congruent with our abilities or level of commitment. The difference between fantasies and possibilities is a fine line, which often may be clearer to an outside observer than our own self-perception. What often makes the difference is our level of determination and willingness to follow through. Many achievements were thought impossible until someone had the vision and discipline to make them happen.

Rage

Rage stores itself primarily in the genital area, the creative center of the body, which defines quite clearly the nature of this emotion. Rage is the holding back of our creative energy. This is often unexpressed sexual energy, but it usually goes beyond this, and frequently, it is our artistic expression that has been thwarted or given away. It may also be our resourcefulness—not claiming that we have the talent and resources to do what we want to do. Often it is the denial of our playfulness, the belief that life should be serious and that play is unnecessary.

Life is designed for our upliftment, learning and growth. Like the game of a child, it commands all of our attention and can be approached with a great sense of empowerment and enchantment. As we grow older, external demands may increase, and it becomes easy to abandon the Inner Child and become overly serious. This usually does not produce a very exciting life for others or us. The alternative is to embrace the Inner Child and create a more joyful life, filled with wondrous adventure and challenges. And everything works better when we remember to have fun!

Opening the pelvis and the throat, the two main centers of sexual and verbal expression, is vital to getting a positive flow of energy moving in these areas. Many genital-urinary disorders are related to rage and can be improved greatly by allowing a freer expression of creativity, resourcefulness, and playfulness. Singing, dancing and a balanced sex life do much to bring this expression out. A good affirmation is: "I am allowing the full expression of my creativity, resourcefulness and playfulness."

Frustration

The emotion of frustration centers itself in the solar plexus. Situated in the pit of the stomach, this center is associated with involvement, the willingness to be present and deal with things as they are right now. Frustration comes when we have a sense that what we want to see happening is not manifesting in the way or at the pace we want it to happen. It is usually based on impatience and an absence of purposeful action.

It often can appear easier to us to be frustrated with circumstances than to honestly look at the situation and decide on a course of action, but deciding what to do and actually taking the next step will restore our feeling of flow and involvement. When frustration is not acted upon, it invariably turns into self-doubt or depression.

Hate

It is fashionable to see hate as the antithesis of love. This is a profound mistake. Love is not an emotion. It is the quintessence of all reality. In other words, love has no antithesis. As a result of deep, repetitive hurt, people often close their hearts and can no longer experience love. Some people can become so entangled with negativity that they are unable to recognize love and may even strike against it. Hate is not the antithesis of love; it is the denial that love can be present, and it is the process of denying that harmony is possible. It is the affirmation of an irreparable difference that cannot be healed. In many, it is so deeply repressed that it is never acknowledged, yet it is a very common emotion.

Because it rejects the possibility of oneness, hate tends to close the heart and destroy any avenue for communication. It promotes a deep feeling of isolation, often accompanied by powerful feelings of guilt and fear. People who hate are alone, separated, alienated. Whether they are aware of it or not, they are dying inside because they are denying the movement of love that heals and harmonizes all things.

Hate is not always global. It may be directed at a specific situation, person or event. Sometimes hate is turned outward creating a barrier between other people and ourselves, societies, the world, or God. Often it is turned inward and attacks our very being, creating a deep sense of isolation. This pattern often appears in people who were abused physically, sexually or emotionally. The denial of their own worth by someone else slowly turned into self-hatred. These people can become so subjugated in their own being that they identify with their abuser and often demonstrate complete collusion with the very person who so profoundly denied them their reality.

Each time we close our heart, we are in fact, declaring that our love is not strong enough to face a certain situation or person. As with all reactive, negative emotions, it is a signal within our consciousness that we are in a state of imbalance and that we need to attend to it. It can call for protective action, because it is often linked with some abuse or sense of abuse. We need to reaffirm the loving, first to ourselves, and then extending the love to the situation until healing has taken place.

Dealing with hate inside of us is also a challenge because hate is so hateful. Most of us were told how powerful hating is from the time we were very young, so when our parents did not give us what we wanted, we tried to hurt them by saying, "I hate you." We also see the devastating effect of hateful actions in the world and become afraid of that feeling inside of us. We know how devastating it can be when it is acted upon in againstness. We must have the courage to move beyond the hate, get down to the hurt, and heal that place so we can bring back the love that is the essence of life. Letting go of guilt associated with hate is also important and a first step toward health, moving away from denial and repression. Hate challenges us to move to a higher level of realization of oneness, which always begins inside. The relationship to love we establish within ourselves can then be extended to traumatic areas in our lives.

It is also important to note that it is often the people with the most sensitive hearts—the ones who so badly want to experience harmony—who harbor feelings of repressed hate. Their sensitivity is often the source of great hurt and their instinctive reaction to the pain increases the sense of loss and isolation of which they are afraid. By discovering the sustaining quality of love inside themselves, they can break free of their dilemma. By reaffirming the flow of love, the trauma often can be healed and harmony restored.

Body Temple

—

Within these walls
of body
lives spirit –
the intangible, inexplicable,
wide expanse of our
divine content
swaddled inside a frame.

And though both
body and spirit
have their rightful place,
a guru stance
unto itself,
they are entwined,
laced together,
righteous and wise,
acting in concert
to teach us
what we have
come here to learn –

the sting of tears,
prick of pain,
ripples of
confusion and knowing,
forgetting and remembering,
all reaching for our attention,
asking for acknowledgment that
Yes, I see you, hear you, feel you,
am present to all that lies
within this holy vessel.

Your soul will always
call to you, guide you
if you are but willing to
greet each beat of your heart,
flash of sensation
as invitation to live
what is already woven into
the marrow of your bones,
a blueprint intentionally placed,
laid with the sole intention of
taking you to higher ground,
revealing all that you are.

Chapter Eight

THE BODY AS A TEMPLE
OF THE SOUL

The Impact of Empowerment on Our Body

~

We could not complete our examination of spiritual empowerment and its influence on healing the Inner Family without talking about the physical body. In the same way as our soul is our particular instrument of connection with the Spiritual, our physical body is our most direct connection with the physical environment. Without our outer senses and neuro-muscular control, we would have little ability to interact with our outer environment.

In our work we look at the body as the meeting place between the internal (our psycho-spiritual state) and the external (the physical environment). The body is directly influenced by the health of the Inner Family and simultaneously affected by all external physical circumstances. The health of the Inner Family is the foundation of our ability to effectively respond to external challenges. These external challenges may include things such as divorce, disease, death of a loved one, sudden change in economic status, family issues, and many more. When we are under a lot of psychological stress, we are more prone to physical disorders. Conversely, when we are physically challenged, we know how hard it is to maintain a positive attitude and personal effectiveness.

In this chapter we will examine the relationship of each member of the Inner Family to specific aspects of the body. We will then examine the magical design of the body and the affinity of each part of the body with a specific quality of the soul.

The Relationship of the Inner Family to the Body

On the physical level, our spiritual alignment is reflected in the heart, the small intestine, and the circulatory system, which animates, nurtures and restores the entire body. The Inner Family supports the body in those functions. The health of each member of the Inner Family will directly influence the health of specific organs as well as the functions of the physical body.

The Inner Mother rules the spleen and stomach and is connected to the function of digestion and absorption and our general sense of wellbeing. The Inner Mother is also associated with the sense organ of taste.

The Inner Father rules the kidneys and the bladder. In the Chinese tradition, the kidneys are the foundation of our life force. The kidneys are also associated with the uro-genital function and the health of the bones, nerves and the hair on top of our head. The Inner Father is associated with the sensory function of hearing.

The Inner Grandparents rule the lungs and the large intestine. The Inner Grandparents are connected to the protection of the body and related to the skin. The sense organ that is related to the Inner Grandparents is the nose.

The Inner Child rules the liver and the gall bladder. The Inner Child is associated with tissue repair, detoxification and the ligaments. The Inner Child is also associated with the sensory function of seeing.

The physical body is the medium through which love—the energy of the soul and the essence of God—can be manifested on the planet. When we are receptive to God, our essential needs are fulfilled and we naturally want to share the abundance with everyone as we realize the oneness in our diversity. When we do this, we can partake of the fruits of the earth in a balanced way. The physical body is also our tool of perception and action. Through the sense organs and our intuition, we can perceive the specific needs of the people, situations and environments that surround us. Through the neuromuscular response of the physical body, we can act upon those needs and demonstrate our loving and commitment to service. When the physical body is in harmony with the soul, it is naturally attuned to the physical functions that support our physical health and the psycho-spiritual functions that support the authenticity of our unique expression.

The Relationship of the Body to the Soul

Each part of the body is attuned to a soul intention that manifests as a quality or qualities that facilitate the equilibrium and the strength of that specific area. These qualities contribute to our overall physical balance and keep us on purpose with our spiritual expression. Let us examine the structure of the physical body and how these qualities reveal our spiritual purpose and function on the planet. We will look at key qualities that correspond to each part of the physical body.

Because the body is a functional instrument helping us be active in our lives, some of the qualities, expressed as words for health and healing, are derived from their logical function as a body part. Other words may seem less obvious but are no less congruent, as they express important aspects of our spiritual expression. I discovered these words intuitively rather than logically, and the explanations came to me after the discovery rather than vice-versa.

One note of interest to many people is that these words have a positive energetic effect in the body whether the person understands them, believes them or interprets them in the same way I do. For example, I have found that when I am working with an English-speaking person with a weakness in the solar plexus, I can use either the English word "involvement" or the French word "engagement" with the same positive results.

In general, reflecting on the words that strengthen and balance the lower extremities, we discover that all these qualities define our *foundation* in the world. From the genitals to the throat, the key words reflect the qualities that facilitate our *movement* in the world. In the head our *relationship to God* is being defined. In the arms, we receive the keys to our *actions* in the world. The key word for each area becomes an energetic tuning fork to the quality that brings movement and transformation in that area.

Each key word can also become a source of reflection on how bringing that quality in that area of our consciousness can alter the way we approach certain situations.

In the following section I look at specific parts of the body and the challenges that are often reflected in these areas. Using the word brings balance into the body and starts shifting the consciousness toward a more positive expression. If you are aware of the weakness associated in this area, it will take consistent repetition of the word and awareness of its potential positive impact in that area for optimal results. For each word, I share with you the positive impact the word can have as a positive influence in that area of your body and your life.

Words for Health and Healing

Feet

The key word is DIRECTING. The feet represent our closest connection to the Earth, and in order to take us anyplace, they need to be focused in the same direction. The negative quality is confusion—being pulled in two directions at the same time, as if each foot wants to go its own way. A typical mental pattern negatively affecting the feet is, "I am on the planet but I don't like it here." This represents our conflict in relation to the planet and a resistance to the Divine Plan. Another pattern is conflict between our inner feelings—our sensitivity, which relates to our left foot—and being active in the world, represented by our right foot. The word directing reminds us that it is our responsibility to choose wisely our course of action in the world and that lack of clear choices clearly aligned with our Divine purpose brings confusion and negative outcomes.

Ankles

The key word is ADJUSTING. The ankle is a highly articulated joint that enables us to adjust to the terrain, no matter how uneven it is, and maintain our standing position. That function in life, on a psychological level, is fundamental. It enables us to go through our day in a world in which things usually are not as smooth and level as we would like them to be. The negative pattern here can be twofold: either rigidity or lack of firmness. In the first case you fight the terrain; in the second you let the terrain lead you and you lose the clarity of your purpose. The word adjusting reminds us to be flexible in the face of challenges and unforeseen circumstances so we can maintain our clarity of purpose and direction.

Calves and Shins

The key word is SUPPORTING. The muscle in the front of the lower leg supports the action of the foot, while the muscles in the back of the lower leg support the function of the knee. Together they hold us in our strength while maintaining flexibility. The negative qualities that can manifest in this area of the body are either lack of self-support when the muscles are flaccid or lack of trust in external support when the calves and shins are rigid and tense. The word supporting reminds us that it is our responsibility to maintain both strength and flexibility when we approach life situation.

Knees

The key word is UNIQUENESS. Verbs such as "revealing" or "actualizing" in relationship to our uniqueness are also powerful adjuncts for this part of the body. The knee is the part that moves forward first when we walk. In the same way, our uniqueness is what we came to express on this planet, and we need to bring it forward. The negative qualities that block this expression are conformity or rebelliousness, resulting from fear and opposition, or resistance, which stems from lack of faith. Distrust and self-doubt resulting from fear also limit this function. The word uniqueness reminds us that we were not designed to fit in a box but are meant to clarify our own course and usher forward our personal contribution.

Thighs

The key word is DETERMINATION. This is the largest, most powerful group of muscles in the body. Whether you are lifting, pushing or pulling, your thighs are your greatest allies. Without the commitment of our strength to our chosen endeavors, we will never know what we are truly capable of. The negative qualities are the stubbornness that supports resistance and the lack of resolve that fosters tentativeness and lack of results. The word determination reminds us that in life nothing comes into manifestation without challenges. It is through our determination that we overcome difficulties and build up the strength to bring forward our contribution.

Hips

The key word is BALANCING. Because the hips include the joint closest to our center of gravity, they are fundamental in the function of balance. When we walk or move, our body shifts weight from one leg to the other, staying balanced due to the action of the hips. In the same way, being balanced in the world is a process of alternately supporting ourselves and allowing the world to support us, as well as moving forward and reaching out to greater potential. If we rely solely on ourselves, we become isolated and our expression is held back, throwing us out of balance. If we depend too much on others, we also lack balance and can easily fall. The word balancing reflects the relationship between the need to support our own expression while we also welcome and embrace the contribution that others can make in our endeavors.

Genitals

The key words are ACCEPTANCE and PATIENCE. At some time in our lives, most of us have had a challenging process in our relationship to sexuality involving denial, shame, confusion, fear, possessiveness or rage. This area can move us to greater and greater levels of unconditional loving if we are simply willing to practice patience and acceptance of ourselves and others. The opposite of acceptance is denial, often associated with the experience of humiliation and feelings of shame. The word acceptance reflects the frequent challenges with life situations not meeting our fantasies, desires and expectations. It is a first step toward transformation. By starting where we are in our expression and being patient with the process we can move forward and use everything for our upliftment, learning and growth.

Buttocks

The key words are ABUNDANCE and ALLOWING. The buttocks are often the place where we were punished as children when we responded to our natural curiosity and desires and got involved in things that displeased our adult entourage. As a result, we tend to hold what we want and what we claim we cannot have—our sense of lack—in our buttocks. If we align our desires with our heart, knowing we can have everything that supports our destiny here, we will naturally allow our creativity, resourcefulness, and playfulness and manifest our abundance.

Lower Belly

The key word is SERVICE. This area of service is usually perceived as the center of power, referred to in various traditions as "hara," "dantian" or "kath." Tension in this area can come from a lack of alignment with the heart, indicating the power is misdirected. It also comes when service is only directed outwardly and an individual is losing power because they are not taking care of themselves. As we align our power with service, we simultaneously eliminate many fears and contradictions regarding power. Our personal power aligns with heart directed service and naturally fulfills our destiny, supporting us in assisting others.

Navel

The key word is FREEDOM. The umbilicus is the channel through which we are nourished in the womb. In our psyche it represents the connection with our mother or a longing for that connection. Dependency and counter-dependency are the common negative patterns connected with this area. The former is claiming, "I cannot be whole without you." The latter says, "Take care of me but do not tell me what to do," a familiar stand in adolescence. Freedom tends to manifest in two forms: freedom "from," reactive and progressively limiting consciousness, and freedom "to," proactive and progressively liberating thoughts, feelings and actions. A key is to recognize that the world is an interdependent system where each part is connected with all others. At the same time, each part holds a unique responsibility to assist in supporting the whole. The word freedom here supports our autonomy while expressing our interdependency.

Upper Belly or Solar Plexus

The key word is INVOLVEMENT. This center is associated with our emotions and is connected to our degree of caring. Negative patterns associated with this area are distinctly different. Over-involvement with others results in our losing our identity; aloofness and lack of caring results from fear of getting involved. Perfectionism also often limits our involvement to those experiences that carry little risk of failure. Our degree and quality of our involvement rules the degree of learning we derive from an experience and guide us through trial and error to discover the balance between taking care of ourselves, others and the world.

Center of the Chest or Heart Center

The key word is PARTICIPATING. The heart energy has to do with oneness and communion. There are two major negative aspects that block the heart. Cynicism lashes out at that which is sacred and beautiful. Over-protectiveness results in our refusal to participate in the dance of life for fear of being hurt. Participating is the realization that in our uniqueness and diversity we are one, all part of a puzzle, each one different yet forming one perfect image. Participating is the action of claiming that we belong; it is our willingness to continue playing the game until we discover our perfect part and learning to play it 100 percent. Another word that opens the heart is GRATITUDE because it recognizes every experience as a Divine gift and fully carries the essence of participation.

Upper Chest or Thymus Gland Area

The key word is SURRENDERING and the quality is COURAGE. To align with the heart and fully express our loving essence, we have to become totally receptive and vulnerable, like little children, and face the unknown. The negative aspects are control, which denies God's love and protection, and cowardice, which denies our inner strength and resourcefulness. To surrender to the heart we have to let go of our need to control and to know before we act. We need to sacrifice the protective mechanism of our ego and embrace our trust and faith in the power of love. That indeed is the ultimate courage.

Throat

The key word is OBEDIENCE. The throat is the center of expression. When our actions are in line with our inner knowing—the voice of the heart—we are in a state of obedience. One state, which often keeps us from expressing the truth of our heart, is the fear of punishment or being ridiculed. When we are run by this fear, we either enter into deceit and betray our truthfulness or simply attempt to become invisible. Obedience to our voice of truth requires standing in our authenticity whatever the consequences and living our life with great integrity.

Mouth

The key word is APPRECIATING. To appreciate is to put the appropriate value on our experiences and the actions of others. Negative aspects that cancel appreciation are disdain, disgust, bitterness and sarcasm. When we focus on the negative, we attempt to belittle everything and everyone, including ourselves. We cannot be constantly critical of others without eventually turning that energy upon ourselves. When we praise rather than criticize, we naturally enhance our positive outlook and diminish any negativity. To look at the cup as half full rather than half empty is not denial; it is just a choice—one of focusing on the positive and helping fill our cup to the brim so we have plenty to share with others.

Nose

The key word is ACKNOWLEDGMENT. It is the action of claiming the totality of who we are: our inner beauty, resourcefulness, creativity, courage and willingness to risk. Common negative aspects are pride, as in being stuck in a position of superiority, false humility and self denial. As we claim that we are God's children, we naturally align with who we truly are, letting go of any antics and false expressions.

Ears

The key word is ATTUNING. Like a radio, we receive many channels and voices calling to us at the same time. As we become attuned to the voice of Spirit within, we are provided with natural guidance. The negative pattern here is spiritual indolence. By not exercising our ability to choose (usually because it requires time and concentration), we are prey to opinions, rumors and innuendo that drain our energy and power of commitment. Being lazy is being tuned to the wrong channel. By becoming more attuned to the voice of the heart, we can learn to recognize what expands or constricts our consciousness. Our power of attunement enables us to choose the music we want to dance by.

Eyes

The key word is FOCUSING. The eyes are very powerful, as they rule a great portion of our perception. Through focusing, we choose our direction then, through our feet, we walk there. Both work to mobilize the will, but vision dictates the direction. If we can't see where we are going, either in reality or in the creative imagination, it is practically impossible to reach a desired outcome. The main limitation affecting this area of the body and its corresponding function is confusion. This is the confusion of not knowing where to focus, being split in our focus through conflicting desires or having a focus so narrow that we miss opportunities. The ability to maintain a clear focus brings clarity and sharpness to our visions and goals.

Center of the Forehead or "Third Eye" Center

The key word is DEVOTION. To be devoted is to let go of judgments and see the Divine presence in all things, all situations and all people, including ourselves. Arrogance blocks devotion with the belief that we know how people or situations should be. As we enter into devotion, we align our focus with God and invoke the Divine Presence and trust that it will manifest to us in a perfect way. Devotion opens the spiritual center in the forehead and allows Spirit to flood our consciousness.

Top of the Head or "Crown" Center

The key word is AT-ONE-MENT. This is the quality of claiming our oneness with God. As we realize that God is love, we become aware that love is the essence of all things. The negative aspects that block this process are lack of understanding and lack of reverence. This leads to not seeing the Divine in all things as opportunities for our upliftment and growth. When we embrace the oneness and demonstrate loving in all aspects of our lives, we become one with the love and one with God.

Hands

The key word is REACHING OUT. Giving and receiving are the movements of love and the expression of the heart. Reaching out represents the willingness to enter into that process. Fear of authority and unworthiness blocks this natural ability. As children, we reached out toward the things that attracted our attention, the objects of our desire, and often we were slapped on the hand for touching things adults had decided we shouldn't handle. As a result, many of us have developed the erroneous belief that we are not supposed to have what we truly want, and we have lost the trust necessary to reach out to God and/or our fellow humans. We have settled for what people were willing to let us have; in the process we have denied our creative abilities. In creating a clear vision for our life and seeing ourselves reaching out for what we truly want, we open up to new expanded possibilities and opportunities.

Wrists

The key word is ARTICULATING. The wrist is the most articulated joint in the body. It enables us to carry out many subtle tasks. In the same manner, in order to allow ourselves to manifest our vision, we need to articulate it in words. The more specific our vision is, the easier it is to express it in words. The better our vision is expressed, the easier it is for us to relate to it and to communicate it to others. The main limitations in this area are confusion and superficiality. Learning how to articulate our goals and projects facilitates our ability to create successful action steps and helps us elicit support from other people.

Forearms

The word is MOBILIZING. Although much of what we do in life involves our hands, the muscles that activate the fingers are in our forearms for the most part. Once our vision has been articulated into clear goals and objectives, we need to mobilize resources. These resources may be internal as they relate to qualities, strengths, talents, skills or assets we already have. They may also involve drawing upon other people's knowledge and abilities. The common limitations are self-doubt, procrastination, fear of making mistakes, fear of rejection and lack of creative thinking. Mobilizing all our inner and outer resources turns fantasy and wishful thinking into reality and practical outcomes in support of ourselves and others.

Elbows

The key words are STYLE and EXTERIORIZING. Many people think of style as what is fashionable. Style is much more than that. It is the exterior manifestation of our uniqueness. It is remarkable that when anyone comes into alignment with his or her style, the heart center always opens up. Doing something that violates our style tends to close our heart, decrease our effectiveness and engender self-doubt. The main limitations are lack of self-confidence, conformity and wanting to draw attention to ourselves or impress others. Defining our style in life starts with an understanding of who we are, rather than how we want to appear. It is self-referenced rather than referenced in the world.

Upper Arms

The key word is PERSEVERANCE. Part of the process of life is to be challenged in our limitations so we can be strengthened in our abilities and resourcefulness. As a result, things we have planned seldom come to us exactly as we had envisioned them or in the timing we had hoped. The people who do not persevere in their efforts tend to get more of what they already have or, worse, gain little knowledge about how to get what they truly want. Perseverance may then reveal itself as a great virtue. To practice an open attitude to the unforeseeable fosters flexibility and promotes a willingness to allow the actions of serendipity. God usually knows better than we do. What is being brought forward to us is even more beautiful than what we could have anticipated. Many times, it is through the process in persevering toward reaching our goals that we master the qualities required to effectively handle the outcomes.

Shoulders

The key word is CONNECTING. Many of us put things into motion without being really connected with them. Our hearts, emotions and thoughts, and the clarity of our images are not aligned with what we are doing. The main limitations in this domain are being pushy, which is a result of a lack of faith or self-trust, and tentativeness, which comes from a lack of commitment. Being pushy tends to interfere with the process and alienates the external support that could be available to us. Our tentativeness betrays us, as it simply does not withstand the test of time. The shoulder connects our arms to the rest of the body.

What we put forward into the world must be an extension of our whole being. All our senses and abilities, clear intentions and commitments must follow through as if they were as precious as our own children. Truly, our expression in the world is unique and deserves all our love and dedication.

Using the Words for Health and Healing to Balance Our Body-Spirit Connection

The Words for Health and Healing are an eloquent example of how the body, mind and Spirit work together as a valuable tool for our upliftment. The key words that bring strength and expansion to major centers in the body point the way to an effective and spiritual way of life. They support our relationship to ourselves, others, God and the world. The repetition of these key words will naturally strengthen the body, the Inner Family and the psyche. They act as models for examining the strengths and weaknesses that are present in our way of life as well as guides for creating specific strategies for change.

Balancing Our Body-Spirit Connection

Try the following exercise to heal your body-spirit connection.

1. Identify an area of pain and weakness in the body.
2. Focus on that area and repeat the key word associated with that area.
3. Create an affirmation to anchor that quality. For example, if the word you identify is "surrender," your affirmation could be: "I am fully surrendering to the support and guidance of Spirit."

Interdependence

—

We are woven into a tapestry
greater than ourselves.
Golden, glistening threads
extending in all directions,
potently unaware
of where we end
and where we begin.
Diving under, over,
starting, stopping,
intersecting, separating,
tightening, loosening,
appearing, disappearing,
in sync with the greater rhythm
as we strengthen our collective ties
through the power of our own
essential filaments.

Chapter Nine

FROM INNER PEACE
TO WORLD PEACE

~~⌒

There are two aspects of peace I am aware of at this time. The first one is an inner experience of peace that appears spontaneously and that tells us of the possibility of ongoing peace. This is what Abraham Maslow referred to as a "peak experience." The second is a strategy for dealing with stress, contradictions, anxiety and limitations. Rather than a state of being, represented by a noun, it is active, as in "peacing" or peacekeeping, an ongoing commitment of awareness and actions toward harmony. I would be very happy if this book helped anyone experience a moment of deep Inner Peace and if, through its influence, people learned how to live more lovingly toward themselves and each other.

Because of the nature of the world, with all of its diversity and the push and pull of our own inner and outer drives, maintaining ourselves in a state of peace is a major challenge. Maintaining peace with our loved ones is no less challenging, and keeping peace in our work environment requires great clarity and dedication. Based on everyday news reports, unresolved social conflicts abound everywhere, and political and international conflicts seem to continually affect our lives in some way.

This book simply suggests that we start the process of peacekeeping within ourselves. This may seem like a cop-out, but I believe that as we become more balanced within ourselves, we will naturally reflect that Inner Peace in our relationships, in the education of our children and in our involvement in the world at large. We will create institutions that are more respectful of spiritual and human values. We will elect leaders who pursue a policy of peace, cooperation, responsibility, mutual respect and understanding.

I am not suggesting a no-action approach to the problems of the world. I believe that many of the issues facing us at the present time are too crucial for us to wait for our perfect inner harmony to lead us into perfect decisions. I am suggesting, however, that we do not approach these issues from the standpoint of blame, guilt, rage, despair and panic, but simply that each one of us begins taking greater responsibility for what we can do.

As I have mentioned throughout this book, I am convinced that there are no good reasons to close our hearts, that this only promotes greater suffering within ourselves and perpetrates the evil of the world. And I certainly do not have the naive belief that it is easy.

The first step I suggest is to commit to keeping love in our hearts toward ourselves and everyone else, regardless of the level of disagreement we may have with their beliefs, attitudes or behaviors. As part of that commitment to loving I believe that forgiveness is a crucial step to moving forward. As long as we are unwilling to forgive ourselves and others for past actions, we are caught up in the past through our righteousness and denial of the possibilities that are open for us here and now.

The four basic movements we explored in this book are critical in maintaining a consciousness of loving on the planet.

- The drive for **preservation** is expressed through caring and is the most fundamental expression of loving. That which we identify with or become one with, we naturally want to protect and take care of. Instead of staying caught in limited identification with our egos or our personalities or the things we are attached to, we need to expand our identity to include everything and everyone. As we do this, caring will become second nature and will become expressed in support of our wellbeing, the welfare of others and the healing of the planet. Through this movement, we will learn to care and to share and to trust in our abundance.

- The drive for **authenticity** is naturally supported through honesty. This implies keeping our word and honoring our commitments. That is the foundation for trust in ourselves as well as in each other. Authenticity also means not getting caught up in dogmas, rigid positions and authoritarianism. The search for truth needs to be aligned with the heart; short of that, it fails to see the beauty of our diversity and wants to enforce a particular version of the truth on everyone. Respect for each other's culture, race, beliefs and traditions is fundamental to the pursuit of peace. As we become more connected with the movement of love, these differences become less and less important. As we affirm the oneness, we grow in tolerance and appreciation.

- The drive for **wisdom** has led us in many new directions in science, medicine, education, spirituality and many other fields of human endeavor. Yet for all that knowledge, we still have people starving all over the world, even in the streets of the most affluent cities. We have allowed our heads to run our hearts, and we are left with the result of our follies. It is time for us to put our heads at the service of our hearts and focus on basic human needs. Our pursuit of objective science has made us look at everything as objects of investigation. However, we are not objects, we are Divine beings, with qualities and abilities that defy scientific inquiries. As each of us aligns our intellect with our heart, the type of knowledge we will bring forward will be aligned with wisdom and will help us understand how to best cooperate with the Divine Plan, rather than try to impose our form of delusion on the universe.

- The drive for **contribution** is the key to creativity. It is predicated on freedom, but freedom without clear direction and discipline is usually dysfunctional. Although rebellion is an important movement toward freedom in an authoritarian context, it is only the first step. Beyond that, we need to create and hold a vision of peace that is unshakeable, and we need to support that vision with all our creativity. We need to honor the uniqueness of each person and child, providing opportunities for growth and mastery, and rewarding work opportunities for the expression of their skills, talents and abilities in service to themselves, others and the world. Let us be as creative about peace as we have been about war, creating a world where everyone has an opportunity for self-fulfillment.

Learning how to bring our Inner Family into a state of balance is the first step in that direction. As we commit to that step, new opportunities are constantly emerging to challenge our loving and expand us beyond our limiting boundaries. The unconditional loving we extend to ourselves reaches our families, professional activities and communities. Let us commit to that first step and meet every new challenge with love. As more people carry peace in their hearts, we will reach a critical mass, the entire world will progressively move into alignment with this new consciousness, and we will all work more cooperatively in resolving some of the key issues facing the planet at this time.

Appendix

OPERATIONAL QUESTIONNAIRE
ABOUT THE INNER FAMILY

~~

The questionnaire below is a reflective exercise which can bring greater awareness about your own Inner Family dynamics. It may be helpful to review the chart on page 51 showing the Positive Expressions of the Inner Family. Use this as an opportunity to assess your level of personal effectiveness on a scale of 0 to 10, with 0 meaning that this expression is not very strong and 10 meaning you are very good at bringing this into your life. Answer the questions as honestly as possible to increase your awareness in these areas.

I. The Mother: Domain of Preservation (Connection)

Respect
- How gentle are you with your own process? ( )
- How gentle are you with other people's process? ( )
- How compassionate are you toward your mistakes or limitations? ( )
- How willing are you to praise yourself for achievements? ( )
- How willing are you to praise others for their achievements? ( )
- How easily do you thank people for what they are doing for you? ( )
- How attentive are you to your needs? ( )

- How attentive are you to other people's needs? ( )
- How easily do your acknowledge your own
  contributions? ( )
- How easily do you acknowledge other people's
  contributions? ( )

Responsibility

- How effective are you at taking care of your needs? ( )
- How good are you at managing your finances? ( )
- How good are you at managing your physical
  environment? ( )
- How reliable are you at taking care of agreed-upon
  tasks? ( )
- How good are you at negotiating responsibilities? ( )
- How willing are you to let other people handle what
  they are able to handle?

Taking Care of Self

Physical

- How effective are you at taking care of yourself
  physically? ( )
- To what degree is your nutrition taking care of your
  needs and promoting health and wellbeing? ( )
- How regularly do you exercise? ( )
- To what degree is your exercise program reflecting your
  need for strength, endurance and flexibility? ( )
- If 7 hours of sleep is a minimum requirement for healthy
  living, to what degree are you achieving this goal? ( )

Emotional

How effectively do you:
- Communicate upsets? ( )
- Communicate needs? ( )
- Make clear actionable requests? ( )
- Creatively handle differences (cooperate)? ( )
- Identify underlying issues? ( )
- Address deeper issues? ( )

Mental

- How effectively do you pursue personal interests? ( )
- How effectively do you seek practical solutions over analysis, theory, diagnosis?
- How satisfied are you with the time you have to reflect? ( )
- How satisfied are you with the amount of time you have to learn new skills? ( )
- How satisfied are you with the amount of time you have to pursue new interests? ( )

Spiritual

How satisfied are you with the amount of time you spend in the following activities:
- Spiritual exercises? ( )
- And/or other spiritual practices? ( )
- And/or Heart-centered meditation? ( )
- And/or contemplation? ( )
- And/or prayer? ( )

Taking Care of Others

- How good are you at approaching others with compassion? ( )
- How good are you at listening to others? ( )
- How good are you at asking others what they need? ( )
- How good are you at trusting other people's ability to take care of themselves? ( )

Service (Beyond the Call of Duty)

- How effectively do you serve your community? ( )
- How effectively do you serve your family? ( )
- How effectively do you serve your friends? ( )
- How effectively to you contribute to maintaining the environment? ( )

II. The Father: Domain of Authenticity (Direction)

Trust / Security

- How much of your security do you place in God? ( )
- How much of your security to you place in material success? ( )
- How much of your security do you place in money? ( )
- How much of your security do you place in being in control? ( )
- How much of your security do you place in knowing what will happen? ( )
- How much of your security do you place in your health? ( )
- How much of your security do you place in others? ( )
- How much do you trust your life to be on track? ( )
- How much do you trust yourself to handle your life? ( )

Commitment / Integrity

- How effectively do you keep agreements with yourself? ( )
- How effectively do you keep your agreements with others? ( )
- How easily do you commit? ( )
- How good are you at course correcting? ( )
- How effectively do you re-negotiate agreement if needed? ( )
- How good are you at following through? ( )
- How clearly do you set your goals? ( )
- How clearly do you identify and track projects? ( )

Clarity

- How clear are you about your life path? ( )
- How clear are you about your spiritual support? ( )
- How clear are you about your spiritual commitment? ( )
- How clear are you about your life purpose? ( )
- How clear are you about your primary relationship? ( )
- How clear are you about your contribution? ( )
- How clear are your goals? ( )
- How effectively do you handle people breaking agreements? ( )
- How clear are you in your requests? ( )
- How clear are you in your boundaries? ( )
- How clear are you in the extent of your involvement? ( )
- How effectively do you make a stand? ( )
- How effectively do you withhold your participation when appropriate? ( )

Tolerance

- How accepting are you of gender differences? ( )
- How accepting are you of religious differences? ( )
- How accepting are you of cultural differences? ( )

- How accepting are you of political differences? ( )
- How accepting are you of things not going your way? ( )
- How accepting are you of generational differences? ( )
- How accepting are you of taste differences? ( )
- How accepting are you of behavioral differences? ( )
- How accepting are you of your own limitations? ( )
- How easily do you forgive? ( )
- How easily do you forget after you forgive? ( )

Leadership
- How effectively do you communicate directions? ( )
- How clear is your vision of possibilities? ( )
- How effectively do you delegate? ( )
- How effectively do you involve others in decision making that concerns them? ( )
- How effectively do you support others? ( )
- How effectively do you allow people to make mistakes? ( )
- How effectively do you deliver feedback? ( )
- How effectively do you clarify that people are on board with your direction? ( )
- How effectively do you clarify goals and outcomes? ( )
- How realistic are your deadlines? ( )

III. The Grandparents: Domain of Wisdom

Zest for Learning
- How much do you enjoy learning? ( )
- How open are you to multiple forms of learning? ( )
- How willing are you to have what you think you know challenged? ( )
- How willingly do you enter into unfamiliar experiences? ( )

- How willing are you to listen to information that does not fit within what you know? ( )
- How willing are you to suspend what you think you know? ( )
- How open and receptive are you to intuitive learning? ( )
- How willing are you to explore experiences out of your comfort zone? ( )
- How willing are you to think out of the box? ( )
- How easily do you look for practical solutions? ( )

Learning from Your Own Experience
- How effectively do you convert experience into wisdom? ( )
- How easily do you turn a mistake into a learning experience? ( )
- How willing are you to design strategies to improve or correct your areas of shortcomings? ( )
- How easily do you participate in new experiences to give yourself opportunities to learn? ( )
- How willing are you to do research when you are aware of a lack of knowledge or competence? ( )
- How willing are you to participate in workshops? ( )
- How willing are you to attend seminars? ( )
- How willing are you to expose yourself to new cultural experiences? ( )
- How willing are you to travel to new countries? ( )
- How willing are you to learn through your body? ( )
- How willing are you to learn relationally? ( )
- How willing are you to validate your hypothesis? ( )
- How willing are you to subject your strategies to the test of outcomes? ( )

Learning from Others

- How willing are you to consult outer sources? ( )
- How willing are you to explore through reading? ( )
- How willing are you to explore through lectures? ( )
- How willing are you to ask for assistance when you do not know? ( )
- How willing are you to learn through CDs or MP3s? ( )
- How willing are you to attend teleconferences? ( )
- How open are you to use learning groups? ( )
- How willing are you to follow a teacher? ( )
- How willing are you to have a mentor? ( )
- How willing are you to receive feedback? ( )
- How willing are you to have others check your assumptions? ( )

Wisdom

- How effective are your life skills? ( )
- How effective are your relational skills? ( )
- How effective are your health skills? ( )
- How often is your experience sought by others? ( )
- How often are others seeking your point of view? ( )
- How frequently are others seeking your competence? ( )
- How often are others inviting your participation in a project? ( )
- How often are younger individuals seeking your advice? ( )
- How frequently are people seeking your presence? ( )
- How much do you trust your own wisdom? ( )

Teaching

- How much do you enjoy sharing your knowledge? ( )
- How good are you at sharing your knowledge? ( )

- How effectively do you organize information? ( )
- How effectively do you integrate information? ( )
- How effectively do you create learning opportunities for others? ( )
- How good are you at formulating Socratic questions? ( )
- How effectively do you share your experience in a way that inspires others? ( )
- How frequently do you create opportunities to share your skills, talents, knowledge, experience and wisdom? ( )

IV. The Child: Domain of Contribution

Generosity
- How openly do you share your talents? ( )
- How willing are you to lend a helping hand? ( )
- How easily do you share your enthusiasm? ( )
- How easily do you share your light-heartedness? ( )
- How willing are you to let others be the center of attention? ( )

Authentic Expression
- Is the way you are presenting yourself reflecting your true expression? ( )
- To what degree are you motivated by your need for attention? ( )
- How often do you change your persona to get what you want? ( )
- How direct are you in your communication? ( )
- Are you willing to face rejection? ( )
- How easily do you acknowledge mistakes? ( )
- How easily do you acknowledge shortcomings? ( )
- How easily do you express your opinions? ( )

Cooperation

- How easily are you cooperating with yourself? ( )
- How easily are you cooperating with things as they are? ( )
- How easily are you cooperating with others? ( )
- How willing are you to volunteer? ( )
- How easily do you follow another person's approach? ( )
- How easily do you let others win? ( )

Freedom of Expression

- How spontaneous are you? ( )
- How adventurous are you? ( )
- How playful are you? ( )
- How willing are you to take calculated risks? ( )

Personal contribution

How would you rate your personal contribution in the following areas:

- Relationships? ( )
- Health? ( )
- Friendships? ( )
- Finance? ( )
- Personal development? ( )
- Professional excellence? ( )
- Spiritual development? ( )
- Creative activities? ( )
- Artistic expression? ( )
- Entertainment/Recreation? ( )

The awareness you have received from this questionnaire may generate change all by itself, or you can go one step further by using the exercises in the book to benefit your own Inner Family.

BIBLIOGRAPHY

∾

THEORY OF HUMAN DEVELOPMENT

General:

Aries, P. *Centuries of Childhood.* New York: Random House, 1962.

Erikson, E. H. *Childhood and Society.* New York: Norton, 1963.

Freud, S. *A General Introduction to Psychoanalysis.* New York: Permabook, 1953.

Maier, H. *Three Theories of Child Development.* New York: Harper & Row, 1978.

Maslow, A. *Motivation and Personality.* New York: Harper & Row, 1954.

Papalia, D. E. and Olds, S. W. *Human Development.* New York McGraw-Hill, 1981.

Skinner, B.F. *The Behavior of Organisms.* New York: Appleton Century, 1938.

Thomas, R. *Comparing Theories of Child Development.* California: Wadsworth, 1979.

Watson, J. B. *Psychology from the Standpoint of the Behaviorist.* Philadelphia: Lippincott, 1919.

Prenatal Development and Birth:

Arns, S. *A Season to Be Born.* New York: Harper and Colophon, 1973.

Flanagan, G. L. *The First Nine Months of Life.* New York: Simon and Schuster, 1962.

LeBoyer, Frederick. *Birth Without Violence.* New York: Knopf, 1975.

Nyhan, W. *The Heredity Factor.* New York: Grosset and Dunlap, 1976.

Righ, R. and Shettles, L. B. *From Conception to Birth.* New York: Harper & Row, 1971.

Infancy and Toddlerhood:

Bower, T. G. R. *A Primer of Infant Development.* San Francisco: Freeman, 1977.

Caplan, F. *The First Twelve Months of Life.* New York: Grosset and Dunlap, 1972.

---. *The Second Twelve Months of Life.* New York: Grosset and Dunlap, 1973.

Hess, S., Thomas, A., and Birch, H. G. *Your Child Is a Person; A Psychological Approach to Parenthood without Guilt.* New York: Viking, 1965.

Evans, R. I. *Jean Piaget: The Man and His Ideas.* New York: Dutton and Co., 1973.

Fraiberg, S. H. *The Magic Years.* New York: Scribner & Sons, 1959

Lamb, M. *The Role of the Father in Child Development.* New York: Willey, 1976.

Lewis, M. *The Origin of Intelligence: Infancy and Early Childhood.* New York: Plenum, 1976.

Piaget, J. *Play, Dreams and Imitation.* New York: Norton, 1951.

---. *The Child's Construction of Reality.* London: Routledge and Kegan, 1955.

---. *The Origin of Intelligence in Children.* New York: International University Press, Inc., 1952.

Reese, H. W. *Basic Learning Processes in Children.* New York: Holt, Rinehart and Winston, 1976.

Schaffer R. *Mothering.* Cambridge, Mass.: Harvard University Press, 1977.

Stern, D. *The First Relationship: Infant and Mother.* Cambridge, Mass.: Harvard University Press, 1977.

Tanner, J. M. *Education and Physical Growth.* New York: International University Press, 1971.

Thomas, A., Chess, S., and Birch, H. S. *Temperaments and Behavior Disorders in Children.* New York: New York University Press, 1968.

White, B. L. *The First Three Years of Life.* Englewood Cliffs, New jersey: Prentice Hall, 1976.

Early Childhood:

Evans, E. *Contemporary Influences in Early Childhood Education.* New York: Holt, Rinehart and Winston, 1975.

Ellis, M. J. *Why People Play.* Englewood Cliffs, New Jersey: Prentice Hall, 1973.

Flavell, J. H. *The Development of Role Taking and Communication Skills in Children.* New York: Wiley, 1968.

Ginott, H. G. *Between Parents and Child.* New York: MacMillan, 1965.

Mussen, P., and Eisenberg-Berg, N. *Roots of Caring, Sharing and Helping.* San Francisco: Freeman, 1977.

Brutten, M., Richardson, S. O., and Margaret, C. *Something's Wrong with My Child.* New York: Harcourt, Brace, Jovanovich, 1973.

Coopersmith. S. *Antecedents of Self Esteem.* San Francisco: Freeman, 1967.

Cox, C. M. *Genetic Studies of Geniuses.* Stanford, California: Stanford University Press, 1926.

Furth, H., and Wachs, H. *Thinking Goes to School.* New York: Oxford University Press, 1975.

Lewis, M., and Rosenbaum, L. *Friendship and Peer Relations.* New York, 1975.

Simon, S. B., and Olds, S. W. *Helping Your Child Learn Right from Wrong.* New York: McGraw-Hill, 1977.

Adolescence:

Erikson, E. *Identity: Youth in Crisis.* New York: Norton, 1968.

Gordon, S. *The Sexual Adolescent: Communicating with Teenagers About Sex.* North Scituate, Mass.: Duxbury Press, 1973.

Inhelder, B., and Piaget. J. *The Growth of Logical Thinking from Childhood to Adolescence.* New York: Basic Books, 1958.

Konopka, G. *Young Girls: A Portrait of Adolescence.* Engelwood Cliffs, New Jersey: Prentice Hall, 1976.

Mead, M. *Culture and Commitment: A Study of the Generation Gap.* New York: Doubleday, 1976.

Minton, L. *Growing into Adolescence.* New York: Parents Magazine Press, 1978.

Muuss, R. E. *Theories of Adolescence.* New York: Random House, 1975.

Tanner, J. M. *Fetus into Man: Physical Growth from Conception to Maturity.* Cambridge, Mass.: Harvard University Press, 1978.

Young Adulthood:

Bernard. J. *The Future of Marriage.* New York: World, 1972.

Bird, C. *The Two Paycheck Marriage.* New York: Rawson, Wade, 1979.

Bolles, R. N. *The Three Boxes of Life and How to Get Out of Them.* Berkeley, California: Ten Speed Press, 1978.

---. *What Color Is Your Parachute?* Berkeley, California: Ten Speed Press, 1989.

Fabe, M., and Wilder, N. *Up Against the Clock.* New York: Random House, 1979.

Hope, K., and Young, H. *Momma: The Sourcebook for Single Mothers.* New York: New American Library, 1976.

Kundsin, R. *Women and Success: The Anatomy of Achievement.* New York: Morrow, 1974.

Lerner, R., and Spanier, G. *Child Influences on Marital and Family Interaction.* New York: Academic, 1978.

Mc Bride, A. B. *The Growth and Development of Mothers.* New York: Harper & Row, 1973.

Sheehy, G. *Passages: Predictable Crisis in Adult Life.* New York: Dutton, 1976.

Midlife:

Anstein, H. *Getting Along with Your Grown-Up Children.* Philadelphia: Lippincott, 1970.

Gould, R. *Transformation.* New York: Simon and Schuster, 1978.

Levinson, D. *The Seasons of a Man's Life.* New York: Knopf, 1978.

Lowenthal, M., Thumber, M., and Chiriboga, D. *Four Stages of Life.* San Francisco: Jossey Bass, 1975.

Rubin, L. *Women of a Certain Age: The Midlife Search of Self.* New York: Harper & Row, 1979.

Troll, L. E. *Early and Middle Adulthood: The Best Is Yet to Be, Maybe.* Monterey, California: Brooks-Cole 1975.

Late Adulthood:

Brown, R. N. *The Rights of Older People*. New York: Avon Books, 1979.

Burnside, I. *Sexuality and Aging*. Los Angeles: University of Southern California Press, 1975.

Butler, R. N. *Why Survive? Being Old in America*. New York: Harper & Row, 1975.

Butler, R. N., and Lewis, M. I. *Sex After Sixty*. New York: Harper & Row, 1976.

Jones, R. *The Other Generation: The New Power of Older People*. New Jersey: Prentice Hall, 1977.

Puner, M. *To the Good Long Life: What We Know about Aging*. New York: University Books, 1974.

Seligman, M. *Helplessness*. San Francisco: Freeman, 1975.

Winctein, G. W. *Life Plans: Looking Forward to Retirement*. New York: Holt, Rinehart and Winston, 1979.

Cousins, N. *Anatomy of an Illness as Perceived by the Patient*. New York: Norton, 1979.

Feifel, H. *New Meanings of Death*. New York: McGraw-Hill, 1977.

Kubler-Ross, E. *Death, The Final Stage of Growth*. Englewood Cliffs, New Jersey: Prentice Hall, 1975.

  On Death and Dying. New York: Macmillan, 1979.

Lerner, G. *A Death of One's Own*. New York: Simon and Schuster, 1978.

Mitchell, P. *Act of Love: The Killing of George Zygmaniak*. New York: Knopf, 1976.

Benson, H. *The Mind-Body Effect*. New York: Simon and Schuster, 1979.

Berne, E. *The Games People Play: The Psychology of Human Relationships*. New York: Grove Press, 1964.

Brigg, J., and Pitt, D. *The Turbulent Mirror: An Illustrated Guide to the Chaos Theory and the Science of Wholeness*. New York: Harper & Row, 1989.

Capra, F. *The Turning Point: Science, Society and the Rising Culture*. New York: Bantam Books, 1982.

Davis, M., and Lane, E. *Rainbows of Life: The Promise of Kirlian Photography*. New York: Harper Colophon, 1978.

Deepak, C. *Quantum Healing: Exploring the Frontiers of Mind-Body Medicine*. New York: Bantam New Age Books, 1989.

Diamond, J. *Life Energy*. New York: Dodd, Mead & Co., 1985.

Gardner, H. *Frames of Mind: The Theory of Multiple Intelligences*. New York: Basic Books, 1983.

Gawain, S. *Creative Visualization*. New York: Bantam Books, 1979.

---. *Living in the Light: A Guide to Personal and Planetary Transformation*. Mill Valley, California: Whatever Publishing, 1986.

Gendlin, E. T. *Focusing*. New York: Bantam Books, 1978.

Harris, T. A. *I'm OK—You're OK*. New York: Avon Books, 1967.

Hay, L. L. *You Can Heal Your Life*. Santa Monica, California: Hay House, 1984.

Helmstetter, S. *What to Say When You Talk to Yourself*. Scottsdale, Arizona: Grindler Press, 1986.

McLean, P. *A Concept of a Triune Brain and Behavior*. Papers presented at Queens University, Ontario, 1969.

Muriel, J., and Jongeward, D. *Born to Win*. New York: A Signet Book, New American Library, 1971.

John-Roger. *Relationships: The Art of Making Life Work*. Los Angeles: Mandeville Press, 1986.

John-Roger, and McWilliams, P. *You Can't Afford the Luxury of a Negative Thought: A Book for People with Any Life-Threatening Illness—Including Life*. Los Angeles: Prelude Press, 1988.

Lad, V. *Ayurveda: The Science of Self Healing*. Santa Fe, New Mexico: Lotus Press, 1984.

Locke, S., and Horning-Rohan, M. *Mind and Immunity*. New York: Institute for the Advancement of Health, 1983.

Locke, S., and Colligan, D. *The Healer Within: The New Medicine of Mind and Body*. New York: A Mentor Book, New American Library, 1986.

May, R. *The Courage to Create*. New York: Norton, 1975.

Miller, R. D. *Psychic Massage*. New York: Harper Colophon, 1975.

Newman, J. W. *Release Your Brakes*. New York: Warner Books, 1977.

Ornstein, R. and Sobel, D. *The Healing Brain*. New York: Simon and Schuster, 1987.

Pelletier, K. R. *Mind as Healer, Mind as Slayer*. New York: Delacorte, 1977. Saint Pierre, G., and Boater, D. *The Metamorphic Technique*. Wiltshire, Great Britain: Elements Books, 1982.

Satir, V. M. *Peoplemaking*. Palo Alto, California: Science and Behavior Books, 1972.

Semigran, C. *One Minute Self Esteem: The Gift of Giving*. Santa Monica, California: Insight Publishing, 1988.

Siegel, B. S. *Love, Medicine and Miracles*. New York: Harper & Row, 1986.

Selye, Hans. *The Stress of Life*. New York: McGraw-Hill, 1978.

Simonton, O. C., and Matthew-Simonton, S., and Creighton, J. *Getting Well Again.* Los Angeles: J. P. Tarcher, 1978.

Thie, J. C. *Touch for Health.* Santa Monica, California: DeVorss & Co., 1973.

Yatri. *Unknown Man: The Mysterious Birth of a New Species.* New York: Simon and Schuster, 1988.

Waitley, D. *Seeds of Greatness: The Ten Best-Kept Secrets of Total Success.* New York: Pocket Books, 1983.

Whitfield, C. L. *Healing the Child Within.* Deerfield Beach, Florida: Health Communications, 1987.

ACUPUNCTURE

Austin, M. *Acupuncture Therapy: The Philosophy, Principles and Methods of Chinese Acupuncture.* Wellingborough, England: Turnstone Press Limited. 1974.

Bergeret, C., and Tetan, M. *Passport Pour la Vie Pour une Medecine Globale Sans Peur et Sans Tabaus.* Paris: Maloine, 1976.

Bergeron, M. *Ciel—Terre—Homme, Le Yi Jing: Introduction a la Metaphysique Chinoise.* Paris: Guy Tredaniel, 1986.

Chanfrault, A. *Traite de Medecine Chinoise.* Angouleme, France: Chanfrault, 1981.

Connelly, D. M. *Traditional Acupuncture, The Law of the Five Elements.* Maryland: The Center for Traditional Acupuncture, 1985.

Darras, J. C. *L'Acupuncture Point par Point. Essentials of Chinese Acupuncture.* Beijing, Similia,1985.

Facundo, J. *Medecine Chinoise: Acupuncture.* Edition Encre, 1985.

Kapchuk, T. *The Web That Has No Weaver.* New York: Congdon & Weed, 1983.

Laurent, D. *La Pratique de la Psychologie Chinoise.* Paris: Guy Tredaniel, 1978.

---. *Precis D'Acupuncture Traditionelle de la Maisnie*, 1987.

Lavier, J. A. *Medecine Chinoise, Medecine Faquelle*, 1973.

Low, R. *The Secondary Vessels of Acupuncture*, New York: Thorsons Publishers, Inc., 1983.

Lupasco, S. *L'Energie et la Matiere Psychique*. Paris: Juliard, 1974.

Mann, F. *Acupuncture: The Ancient Chinese Art of Healing and How It Works Scientifically*. New York: Random House, 1973.

Maspero. *Le Taoisme et Les Religions Chinoises*. Paris: Gallimard, 1971.

Paul, M., and Paul, P. *Le Chant Sacre Des Energies*. France: 1983.

Requena, Y. *Acupuncture et Psychologie*. Paris: Maloine, 1982.

---. *Terrains et Pathologie en Acupuncture*. 2 vols. Paris: Maloine, 1982.

Sanchard, P. E. *Les Voies Royales de la Guerison, Acupuncture Homeopathie-Meziere*. Paris: Maloine, 1980.

Soulie de Morant, G. *L'Acupuncture Chinoise*. 2 vols. Paris: Maloine, 1982.

Precis de la Vraie Acupuncture Chinoise. Paris: Mercure de France, 1963.

Schatz, J., Larre, C., and Rochat de La Vallee, E. *Les Energies du Corps*. Milan, Italy: So-Wen s.a.s., 1979.

Tao Te Ching. Translated from the Chinese by Ch'u Ta-Kao. London: Mandala Books, Unwin Paperbacks, 1982.

Timon, A. *L'Equilibre Rythme: La Tradition Chinoise au Service de la Bio-Energetique Humaine*. Paris: Maisonneuve, 1980.

Van Nghi, N. Hoang Ti, Nei King and So Ouenn. (*The Yellow Emperor's Classic of Internal Medicine*). France: Nguyen Van Nghi, 1973.

Weith, I. *The Yellow Emperor's Classic of Internal Medicine*. Berkeley, California: University of California Press, 1972.

LOVE AND THE TRANSFORMATIONAL PROCESS

Anderson, W. T. *The Upstart Spring: Esalen and the American Awakening.* Reading, Mass.: Addison-Wesley, 1983.

Berne, E. *Games People Play: The Psychology of Human Relationship.* New York: Grove Press, 1964.

Berrigan, D. *Love and Love at the End.* New York: MacMillan, 1968.

Gaylin, W. *Caring.* New York: Knopf, 1976.

Bloomfield, H. H. *The Achilles Syndrome: Transforming Your Weakness into Strength.* New York: Random House, 1985.

Buber, M. *A Believing Humanism, My Testament 1902-1965.* New York: Simon and Schuster, 1967.

Buscaglia, L. *Living, Loving and Learning.* Thorofare, New Jersey: Charles B. Slack, Inc., 1982.

---. *Love.* Thorofare, New Jersey: Charles B. Slack, 1972.

Butterworth, E. *Life Is for Loving.* New York: Harper & Row, 1973.

Cardenal, E. *To Live Is to Love.* New York, Herder and Herder, 1972.

Coleman, A. D. *Love and Ecstasy.* New York: Seabury, 1975.

Cousins, N. *The Human Option: Autobiographical Notebook.* New York: Norton, 1981.

Daniels, V. and Horowitz, L. J. *Being and Caring.* San Francisco: Book Co., 1976.

Dathne, R. *Love Until It Hurts* (on Mother Theresa). San Francisco: Harper & Row, 1981.

Drastch, D. R. *Growth to Selfhood: The Sufi Contribution.* Boston: Routledge and Kegan, 1980.

Fromm, E. *The Art of Loving.* New York: Harper & Row, 1956.

Gaylin, W. *Caring.* New York: Knopf, 1976.

Hartman, F. *The Life and the Doctrine of Philipus Theophrastus, Bombast of Hohenheim, Known by the Name of Paracelsus.* New York: John W. Lovell Co., 1963.

Hesburgh, T. M. *The Human Imperative: A Challenge for the Year 2000*. New Haven: Yale University Press, 1974.

Hodge, M. B. *Your Fear of Love*. New York: Doubleday, 1967.

Holmes, M. *Lord, Let Me Love*. Boston: G. K. Hall, 1979.

Hutschnecker, A. D. *Hope: The Dynamics of Self Fulfillment*. New York: Putnam, 1981.

Huxley, L. A. *Between Heaven and Earth: Recipe for Living and Loving*. New York: Farrar, 1963.

Jampolsky, G. G. *Good Bye Guilt: Releasing Fear Through Forgiveness*. New York: Bantam Books, 1985.

---. *Teach Only Love*. New York: Bantam Books, 1983.

Keen, S. *To a Dancing God*. New York: Harper & Row, 1970.

Keyes, K. S. *Handbook to Higher Consciousness*. Berkeley, California: Living Love Center: 1975.

Kiev, A. *Active Loving: Discovering and Developing the Power to Love*. New York: Crowell, 1979.

Kopp, S. E. *Even a Stone Can Be a Teacher: Learning and Growth from the Events of Everyday Life*. Los Angeles: J. P. Tarcher, 1985.

Kreeft, P. *Love Is Stronger Than Death*. San Francisco: Harper & Row, 1979. Krishnamurti, J. *Commentaries on Living*. Theosophical Publication, 1956-1960.

Lasswell, M. *Styles of Loving: Why You Love the Way You Do*. New York: Doubleday, 1980.

Madow, L. *Love: How to Understand and Enjoy It*. New York: Scribner's, 1982.

May, R. *Love and Will*. New York: Norton, 1969.

McNamara, W. *The Human Adventure*. New York: Doubleday, 1974.

Merton, T. *Love and Living*. New York: Farrar, Strauss and Giroux, 1979.

Montagu, A. *Touching: The Human Significance of the Skin*. New York: Columbia University Press, 1971.

---. *The Direction of Human Development.* New York: Hawthorn Books, 1970.

---. *The Practice of Love.* Englewood Cliffs, New Jersey: Prentice Hall, 1975.

Peck, M. S. *The Road Less Traveled: A New Psychology of Love, Traditional Values and Spiritual Growth.* New York: Simon and Schuster, 1978.

---. *People of the Lie: The Hope for Healing Human Evil.* New York: Simon and Schuster, 1983.

Roger, C. *A Way of Being.* Boston: Houghton Mifflin, 1980.

---. *Person to Person: The Problem of Being Human: A New Trend in Psychology.* Lafayette, California: Real People Press, 1967.

Singer, I. *The Nature of Love: Plato to Luther.* New York: Random House, 1966.

Solomon, R. C. *Love, Emotions, Myth and Metaphor.* New York: Doubleday, 1981.

Staples, L. O. *The Four Loves.* New York: Harcourt, Brace, Jovanovich, 1960.

Tennow, D. *Love and Limerance: The Experience of Being in Love.* New York: Stein and Day, 1978.

Teresa, Mother. *The Love of Christ.* San Francisco: Harper and Row, 1982.

Wiener, N. *The Human Use of Human Beings: Cybernetics and Society.* Da Capo Press,1988.

Williams, D. *The Spirit and the Form of Love.* New York: Harper & Row, 1968.

Wolf, F. A. *Star Wane: Mind, Consciousness, and Quantum Physics.* New York: Macmillan, 1984.

BERTRAND BABINET, PHD

Bertrand Babinet, PhD, holds a doctoral degree in Human Development. He is a licensed acupuncturist in Colorado and a world renowned intuitive healer. He has lectured and taught on several continents. His work uses the power of love to release the bonds of the past and promote a life of peaceful harmony.

To learn more: babinetics.com

Poetry

KIMBERLY JONAS

Kimberly Jonas has been facilitating individuals and groups in the exploration and cultivation of the body's innate wisdom for over fifteen years, with her poetry acting as guide and inspiration. A Reiki Master and founder of BodyMantra, Kimberly is known for her ability to facilitate deep and lasting transformation.

To learn more: kimberlyjonas.com

CPSIA information can be obtained
at www.ICGtesting.com
Printed in the USA
FFHW021101041119
55888408-61768FF

9 781732 677609